Create
Your Own
Reality

Create Your Own Reality

A Seth Workbook

Nancy Ashley

Prentice-Hall, Inc., Englewood Cliffs, New Jersey 07632

Library of Congress Cataloging in Publication Data

Create your own reality.

Includes index.
1. Spirit writings.   I. Title.
BF1301.A73   1984   133.9′3   84-4723
ISBN 0-13-189135-9
ISBN 0-13-189127-8 (pbk.)

3 4 5 6 7 8 9 10

ISBN 0-13-189135-9

ISBN 0-13-189127-8 {PBK.}

Editorial/production supervision
and book design: Joe O'Donnell Jr.
Cover design © 1984 by Jeannette Jacobs
Manufacturing buyer: Pat Mahoney

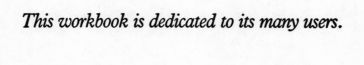

This workbook is dedicated to its many users.

Contents

Acknowledgments

Many thanks to Sue Watkins for giving me permission to use material from *Conversations with Seth* and for her enthusiastic comments and suggestions; to Robert Butts for encouraging me to go ahead with this and for passing on my ideas to Tam Mossman; to Jane Roberts for her interest in the project and for her permission to use the ideas and words from so much of her work; and, of course, to Seth for his guidance throughout the writing of this book.

The author acknowledges the addition of excerpts from the following:

"The God of Sue" is from the book *The God of Jane: A Psychic Manifesto*, by Jane Roberts and Robert F. Butts. © 1981 by Jane Roberts. Published by Prentice-Hall, Inc., Englewood Cliffs, New Jersey 07632.

Conversations with Seth, Volume I, by Susan M. Watkins. © 1980 by Susan M. Watkins. Published by Prentice-Hall, Inc.

Dialogues of the Soul and Mortal Self in Time, by Jane Roberts. © 1975 by Jane Roberts and Robert F. Butts. Published by Prentice-Hall, Inc.

The God of Jane: A Psychic Manifesto, by Jane Roberts. © 1981 by Jane Roberts. Published by Prentice-Hall, Inc.

The Individual and the Nature of Mass Events: A Seth Book, by Jane Roberts and Robert F. Butts. © 1981 by Jane Roberts. Published by Prentice-Hall, Inc.

The Nature of Personal Reality: A Seth Book, by Jane Roberts. © 1974 by Jane Roberts. Published by Prentice-Hall, Inc.

The Nature of the Psyche: Its Human Expression, by Jane Roberts. © 1979 by Jane Roberts. Published by Prentice-Hall, Inc.

The Seth Material, by Jane Roberts. © 1970 by Jane Roberts. Published by Prentice-Hall, Inc.

Seth Speaks: The Eternal Validity of the Soul, by Jane Roberts. © 1972 by Jane Roberts. Published by Prentice-Hall, Inc.

The Unknown Reality, Volume I, by Jane Roberts. © 1977 by Jane Roberts. Published by Prentice-Hall, Inc.

A Personal
Preface

When I first met Seth a decade ago, I thought he was a fake. One evening, a young girl I'd just met dropped by, full of high energy from a yoga class, with a purple-covered paperback under her arm. *Seth Speaks* was its title, and one look at the picture on the cover told me all I needed to know. Here was some woman in trance, supposedly receiving the words of some spirit from some other dimension.

What nonsense! No self-respecting college teacher like me was about to be taken in by *that* kind of stuff. There was plenty of it around, and the girl, Kathy (who said she was a psychic), read it all. I wondered once again why it was that I liked her so much. Though she, at seventeen, was the same age as my son, ours was not a parent-child attraction. This new-found friendship was odd, coming as it did during a time in my life when I felt estranged from my longtime friends and from the world I'd once felt part of.

Three years before, I had gone away for a year's sabbatical in Spain with my son and daughter. It was my first experience with singleparenting responsibilities, my first time to travel extensively, my first in-depth knowledge of another culture. I had expected my life to be different during that year away, and it certainly was. But I hadn't expected that on returning to the familiar world of Hawaii, where I'd made my life since 1960, it *too* would seem entirely different, as if I were still in a foreign country. At the time it didn't occur to me that *I* had changed, for I still felt like the same person—a new single parent with a sabbatical under her belt; but other than that, no different from before.

I was no longer a "woman-in-relationship-to-a-man," and once back home, I hadn't expected that to have much effect on my life. But I soon found it did affect the choices available to me—my social life, the way I saw others— as if, in all my life until then, I hadn't really had an independent existence. Now that I did, I wasn't sure how I liked it.

Another difference was in my attitude toward my college teaching. While in Spain, I had outlined a textbook for writing students—one of many I'd developed over the years of teaching at the University of Hawaii—and it had been accepted for publication. But when I got back and resumed work on it, I found I no longer believed the premises it was based on. In fact, I found that I no longer believed many of the premises I'd held about the teaching and learning of writing. I even doubted that students *could* learn to write through using a book. But if that were the case, how was I to justify my existence?—for that existence, I felt, had been justified by being published.

1

Not only did my newfound independence and job feel strange to me, so too did my friends. Here they were, voicing the same concerns they'd been voicing before I left, as if that year away had never happened. It made me uncomfortable that they were just the same—I no longer could work up much enthusiasm for their interests, yet at the same time, I was inarticulate about my own. At least this girl Kathy's strange interests were fresh and new to me. Certainly I didn't believe in astrology and reincarnation, which she talked about in such a matter-of-fact way; but then again, I no longer knew *what* I believed any more.

While in this frame of mind—shortly after Kathy came by with the Seth book I didn't read—I decided to take a year's leave of absence from the university and go to California, where I had lived before Hawaii, one of the few places in the U.S. I could find a climate warm enough for my thin Hawaiian blood. By going somewhere else, I thought, perhaps I could get a perspective on life that I couldn't seem to get in Hawaii. Here I was, flailing around with all the classic symptoms of a mid-life crisis and had to do something about it—take some time away to mull over the changes I was going through.

One thing had become clear to me; I wanted to become a "writer." For some years I'd spent many hours a week writing, but as far as I was concerned, the articles and textbooks I'd published weren't "real writing." To be a writer you had to write *fiction*, and that was what I now proposed to do.

So I took a year's leave from my job, and left for California with my eleven-year-old daughter and vague notions of finding a quiet place to write and, at the same time, sort out my existence. But there was also the matter of supporting us while doing so. After staying with friends across the bridge from San Francisco for a few days, I realized that Marin county was far too expensive for a salaryless writer-to-be and her hearty daughter.

Then someone just happened to mention that Sonoma county, adjacent to Marin to the north, was a cheaper place to live. So one gloriously crisp sunny day, we just happened to drive up that way, past Santa Rosa and into a forest of giant redwoods to the west. Struck by the majestic beauty of those trees, we decided to look for a place to live in that area. We just happened to see a notice on the bulletin board of a small country store, made a phone call, and within an hour had rented a tiny low-rent cabin in Monte Rio, in a redwood grove by the rushing Russian River.

Strangely enough it also happened that both our landlords were writers, supporting their habit off the revenue from their clump of cabins. The wife was in a women writers' group, which to this day is going full steam in nearby Guerneville. We became instant friends, and she dragged me to the group figuratively kicking and screaming—after all, what business did I have there when I wasn't a writer? But after my first meeting of the writer's group I was hooked—not on the writing so much as on interacting with the most fascinating, colorful women I had ever met.

2

In Hawaii I had always thought my life style somewhat bohemian compared with that of my colleagues at the university. But here, ensconced smack in the middle of counter-culturedom, I felt straight as a pin. I always felt self-conscious when I went into the local health food store. I would invariably be the only one clad in jeans and a sweater and not a hippie costume. Somehow these people managed to keep themselves housed, clothed, and fed through bartering, swapping, part-time jobs, and food stamps. Many were artists of some kind, and all were avid about at least one thing, be it the women's movement, building a house, the school system, nutrition, or zen. Of course, I saw them with very much the same romantic eye as I had observed the villagers in the small Spanish town where we'd lived on sabbatical. But these were compatriots who spoke the same language (sort of) and, for the most part, came from the same middle-class roots. During the year I got to know many of them quite well and formed a number of lasting friendships.

There we were, then, my daughter and I, living in a miniature cabin under gigantic trees in a hippie community. Most days I spent at the desk I'd devised from a door and orange crates tucked into the six-by-eight-foot kitchen. The oven warmed my back while my daughter lolled her days at the nearby, low-pressure school, across the river by the bridge. But this was not my year to write the Great American Novel; other than a handful of short stories, the writing I did turned out to be largely self-exploratory. It was quite exhilarating—the powerful setting, getting to know these people, my embryonic attempts at fiction—yet I was still sad much of the time, as if in mourning for an old self I no longer was. In writing about my past, I came to see that I had heretofore sought, unsuccessfully, a sense of direction through matehood; now it was entirely up to me to find direction in my life—which made me feel lonely. Also, I came to see I'd been something of a prima donna at my job, with more interest in being a star than concern for my students— which made me feel insecure about going back to teaching. Then again, here I was living with people, some of them as weird as Kathy, who believed in all sorts of off-the-wall things and weren't doing what they were "supposed" to in terms of holding full-time jobs and keeping money in the bank. They were so damned vibrant and colorful and appealing, yet they and I were worlds apart ... or were we?

The year in Monte Rio, then, did *not* help me sort things out, so much as make me aware of what I had been and wasn't any more. Having glimpsed that my year in Spain had given me a different view of reality, I could never be the same person again. Spending yet another year in a "foreign" culture changed me some more. Through viewing those who had different beliefs (and thus a different reality) my own beliefs became visible and unacceptable—by contrast. I had to cast them aside, but didn't know what to replace them with.

It was at this point that I met Seth for the second time. Preparing to leave my forested setting for Hawaii and the university, I stopped by a friend's to say goodbye when she just happened to be reading *Seth Speaks*. After a year midst all these people, I was more broad-minded and curious than when I'd arrived. I opened the book toward the middle, and read, "If you expand your sense of love, of health, and existence, then you are drawn in this life and in others toward those qualities; again, because they are those upon which you concentrate. A generation that hates war will not bring peace. A generation that loves peace will bring peace [*Seth Speaks*, p. 197]."

What was so far out about *that* idea? I wondered. It made sense to me. I glanced quickly at different passages through the book—for this was not the occasion for reading it—and was particularly struck by its clarity and coherence, and the authenticity I sensed behind it. In the past, I'd looked through "esoteric" books and found it difficult to get past the prose, whatever their potential merit. But this I found clearly written, easy to understand, and "right on," as Kathy had said. This Seth really spoke to me!

On returning to Hawaii, I bought all the Seth books then published— *The Seth Material, Seth Speaks,* and *The Nature of Personal Reality*. First I read them through, underlining parts and writing notes in the margin. Then I went back and began doing some of the exercises suggested, writing in my journal about what happened. Soon I'd established a daily routine of "Sethitations," as I called them, that were to become the main focus of my life for about three years. I became something of a recluse, leaving my house only to go to the university or to the beach a half block away. The rest of the time I spent at home, mostly alone. Creating a new reality for myself was my goal and Seth my trusty guide.

At first I'd resisted his key idea, that we create our own reality, because at that time, there were many aspects to my reality that I didn't like. Why would I have created them? But then I began to look on the positive side and see all the pleasant aspects of my reality. I began to appreciate myself for what I had done *right* and saw an important implication in the idea: if we do create our own reality, then we can make whatever changes we want. We are in control of our destiny! I saw how helpless I had felt, thoroughly believing that "outside forces" were making me behave the way I did, that I didn't *have* control. So this new idea was quite a revelation to me.

Over the years I had done a lot of reading in psychology. In the early sixties I'd discovered Maslow, who then spoke to me as meaningfully as Seth spoke a decade later. Maslow believed we should look to healthy, self-actualizing people as models to emulate, rather than to deficient, needful people as models of what *not* to be like. That made eminent sense to me. His description of self-actualizing people was inspiring, but it hardly seemed possible to become a person like that. I couldn't just *will* myself to have a feeling of wholeness and interconnectedness with all others, spontaneity, openness and honesty, benevolence, individuality, autonomy, playfulness, and on and on. People who had such qualities must have been born with them, or had a much different childhood from mine and, for that matter, from most people. After all, the psychology books said that we're molded by age six; that it is incredibly difficult to change that mold—and so the best you can do is to adjust to the who you are—a static, fixed model.

But from Seth, I got the notion that we're not at the mercy of our past; that we can *always* change our reality through changing our beliefs; that we can create the reality we want simply by believing in it. Doing this is a matter of discovering *conscious* beliefs that stand in the way of creating this new reality and then replacing these beliefs with constructive new ones. If those beliefs are invisible to us, it's because we take them for granted as assumptions underlying our reality—not because they are buried somewhere in the unconscious mind. (And according to Seth, the "unconscious"—that part of our mind that's tuned into the cosmos—is much *more* conscious than our so-called conscious, ego-dominated mind; and just as organized, but in a different way.)

Once I came to the emotional realization that we're not at the mercy of our past or of an unfathomable unconscious, I was on my way. As if I'd turned a corner in my mind, whatever happened to me after that I viewed in a new light. Something I would have labeled "bad" before, I now looked at as simply evidence of a belief I hadn't been aware of. Now that I was, I could change it. With this new awareness, I no longer felt the need to hassle myself about "bad" things I'd done. I could see why I'd done them—what beliefs were operating—and could thus be more tolerant of myself for doing them. Increased self-esteem and confidence led, in turn, to new revelations, new changes, more confidence—a snowballing effect. Often I wrote in my journal of being in a cocoon-like state, building a butterfly from beliefs, and I used the same metaphor as I moved out of the cocoon and went into the world once more.

As time went on, it struck me how much more vivid the world seemed to be. I went hiking one day on a trail I hadn't traveled for years. I remembered it as a gloomy path, but this day it was glowing with color and seemed pulsing with energy. I've seen it that way every time since, and it's almost incomprehensible that I could have viewed the trail in any other way. And yet I had created a gloomy reality for myself—on that trail, and in other aspects of my life.

Today, all that has changed. I can't remember ever having felt depressed in the past five years. My mood changes from euphoric—much of the time—to mildly impatient—when my beliefs don't take effect fast enough. I have become most comfortable with my independence, loving the sense of competence when I overcome obstacles, solve problems, or venture into the unknown. My work at the university has totally changed. I never "give lectures" any more, but have made seminars out of my classes with the students running the show, keeping myself as far in the background as I can get. Through this method, I quite naturally came up with a new idea for teaching materials that I wrote up in the form of a workbook for writing students, which is soon to be published.

My friends nowadays come in many varieties, reflecting my more diversified interests and increased tolerance for many points of view. Having become increasingly attuned to nature and in harmony with its deep rhythms, I have arranged my living environment to take full advantage of its soothing influence. My oceanfront cottage at Mokuleia on Oahu's rural north shore,

5

looks out at crashing seas framed by palms, and has the natural ventilation of trade winds wafting through screen windows. As I write this, I am viewing the verdant green mountains behind the cottage. My artwork covers the walls. I had been dabbling in art for years but had never been satisfied with my results. Then one day, after months of examining my beliefs about the nature of my creativity, I hit upon a sort of bas-relief in cloth—a medium of expression that's just right for me and expresses a strong sensuality that hadn't emerged in anything I wrote. I began turning out pieces regularly and now they have begun to attract interest and buyers.

So *many* new developments have taken place since I started consciously creating my own reality. One day on the beach I was rereading *The Nature of the Psyche* (I'll never be through learning from those books), and an impulse came to me, which I immediately wrote down in the margin of the book—for I have come to trust my impulses. I wrote: "A Seth Workbook." The next day I got off a letter to Jane Roberts proposing that I do a workbook to go along with the Seth books, and outlining what I intended to do. Within two weeks, I got back a letter saying that I had a good idea there, and to write directly to Prentice-Hall, which I did. The rest, as they say, is history.

The purpose of this long and unabashedly self-congratulatory account is to illustrate that we *do* indeed create our own reality, and can change it if we do not find it to our liking. Of course, as Seth points out, our reality constantly changes anyway, but we can have more of a conscious part in those changes if, first of all, we believe that we can and, second of all, work at it. In retrospect I can see how I was creating my reality all along; how choices I made along the way were necessary prerequisites to developing my *present* reality. If I hadn't read Maslow, for instance, I might not have been ready for Seth later. If Kathy hadn't exposed me to the Seth book a year before, my reaction might have been different when I encountered it a year later. If I hadn't already had experience in writing workbooks, perhaps it wouldn't have occurred to me to do one for the Seth books.

We are continually making choices among actions which then lead us in one direction or another. Our inner self is always trying to guide us toward optimum development of our potentialities, but because we have learned to doubt or mistrust our impulses, because we don't believe in our Selves any more, we often end up dissatisfied, confused, or in a full-blown identity crisis, as I was. Through taking conscious charge of our lives, we can regain the trust and confidence that is everyone's birthright. I am a happy person today; happy with the direction I chose; happy that I did so consciously; happy I "discovered" in Seth someone who could help me. It is out of my positive regard for the Seth teachings that this workbook is conceived. I would like to share my process with others in hope that they too can benefit from it.

In some ways, this book is a distilled version of the course I put myself through. My belief is that, if you do these exercises thoroughly and faithfully, you will gain in a few months' time what I gained, on a hit-and-miss basis over a period of three years. I have done all the exercises in one form or another, and for me, some of them worked better than others. I felt more comfortable doing the more "rational" ones such as the belief assignments, for they were in keeping with my expectations of how one acquires learning. Even so, I think I may have got more out of the more "intuitive" exercises that stretched my imagination and visualizing powers. In most exercises I have tried to combine both the rational and the intuitive ways of learning.

Before going through these exercises, get a thick and sturdy notebook to use as a journal, for this will be an important record of your progress. In these exercises, I have tried my best to summarize as accurately and succinctly as possible many of Seth's broad-reaching ideas. In order to go through this workbook, it isn't necessary to buy any of the Seth books, but, for those who prefer to get it straight from Seth, I have included the sources of my materials.

This workbook would be most useful in a group situation. Many of the exercises can be done together in a workshop setting; others can be done individually and then shared with the group. A group is valuable not only because of the different points of view, but also because it provides motivation. When you know the group is expecting you to have done a particular assignment, you have additional incentive not to put it off.

If you can adopt a playful attitude toward doing these exercises rather . than looking on them as a daily chore you've got to fit in somehow, then you will progress faster and have more fun in the process. But whatever your attitude, it is absolutely necessary that you *do the exercises*. Reading about them is not sufficient! To become a conscious reality-creator takes practice. This workbook will get you started—then it's up to you to keep it up and to integrate the concepts and actions into your everyday existence.

Have fun!

1

The Creation
According to Seth:
Where We Come from

...there is nonbeing. It is a state, not of nothingness, but a state in which probabilities and possibilities are known and anticipated but blocked from expression.

Dimly, through what you would call history, hardly remembered, there was such a state. It was a state of agony in which the powers of creativity and existence were known, but the ways to produce them were not known.

This is the lesson that *All That Is* had to learn, and that could not be taught. This is the agony from which creativity originally was drawn, and its reflection is still seen [*The Seth Material,* p. 264].

It started with a Consciousness desirous of expressing Itself. All That Is—a gestalt of aware-ized energy powered by love—was in a state of latency. It was aware of all Its potentialities, but did not know how to express them. Its imagination knew no bounds; in Its thoughts were universe upon universe of riches. Within It, entities took on ever more vivid form and cried out for realization, for Being. But All That Is did not know how to bring about their actualization, for each of the entities was a thought in Its mind, and each thought a particle of energy. How could It express these thoughts without giving up that portion of energy that formed them?

This was the dilemma of All That Is—an insoluble one it seemed, for it meant separating them from Itself. Yet how could this be? Unity was All That Is. As the agony grew, as all the desirous significance-seeking energy within All That Is sought to deal with the creative dilemma, an idea took form in Its mind. An entirely new concept came to this ageless entity, dimly felt at first, but as its significance grew, so did the feeling behind it: the concept of Separateness-Within-Unity.

Aha! With what longing All That Is imagined the possibilities springing from this new idea. Why, this would allow each of Its envisioned parts to become a being in its own right, as well as a part of It. Each provided with a perspective of its own, different each from the other, viewing life each from its own center. Just think of all It would learn from these beings! They could tell

It what life was like from *their* viewpoints, could show It world upon world of masterpieces through their eyes, adding dimensions to Its existence while learning the dimensions of All That Is. Separateness-Within-Unity—what a splendid idea!

All That Is felt Its entire being hum with the desire to fulfill the possibilities of that significance, to specify that latency, and to give it actuality. Its hum became a high-pitched multi-colored intensity of unbearable longing energized by the entities of All That Is's creation, struggling to break free. Then in an enormous gesture of trust and surrender, All That Is let go. It gave up the idea of limits built in Its mind, and in so doing, set into action the energy that idea had hemmed in.

In the resulting explosion of creativity, psychic universes were seeded, each seed an indivisible bit of aware-ized energy with its own unique perspective and filled with the same exuberant desire to know and to love that had given it birth. Propelled into the constant action of being through memory of the agony of that cosmic dilemma preceding its birth, each seed was aware of the Source which had set it free yet of which it remained a part.

Their emotional desire to create led these seedling consciousness units to combine playfully in myriads of ways. Where they found an organization of significance to them, they built on it, and attracted others of like mind to join them. Thus entire systems of reality were created, arising out of deep abiding feeling, rich in love and the desire to create, constantly in motion.

And so it was that our own physical universe was made manifest. In much the same way that All That Is in Its yearning gave up parts of Itself that they might seek independent existence, so too did some of these parts, in *their* intense yearning for material experience, impress themselves into matter. Giving off an illuminating light everywhere at once, they thus created a medium for life as we know it, the blueprint and tools for all possible life forms.

The stuff of our life, then, is born out of intense emotional desire. It rises naturally from consciousness, carrying perceptions into the material plane on deep feeling-tones of energy, like musical chords of infinite variety. Each of us has our own unique feeling-tone rising up out of the atoms and molecules that form us and casting our own stamp of identity on material existence. These feeling-tones pervade our being and determine the emotional cast that life has for us. They are the connective between us and all others, for they represent the vital force, the raw material from which all being is made. We may have our emotional ups and downs as we react and respond to what happens to us, but beneath these transitory emotions are the long, deep rhythms that underlie the events in our lives, that provide us with direction and purpose, that determine the quality of our perceptions and what is important to us. Feeling-tones are the voice of our soul, representing the essence of our being from which we form our physical experience, the expression of ourself in pure energy, our never-to-be duplicated identity in the flesh. And at the same time, they are our resonating connection with all other beings in three-dimensional existence.

We create our own reality. This first exercise is a basic one, for it gets you in touch with your own unique energy, that portion of All That Is that is manifest in you. In perceiving that energy—that deep musical chord within you—you come to realize that you do have the power to impress your own Self upon the universe, and to realize that that Self is indeed like no other.

Sit quietly and close your eyes. Sense the deep rhythms within you. Try not to have a preconceived notion of what these will be like, but simply look within and wait for those feeling-tones to become apparent to you. You know that these feeling-tones exist, that we are born out of these deep tones, out of the intense desire of All That Is to know Itself through the flesh. You are a unique expression of this feeling, of this desire to Be in the flesh. You are a unique combination of perceptions, inclinations and intents expressing your Self in this three-dimensional world. Open yourself to what you are, and sense those deep tones within you. Become aware of the rhythm of yourself, of the great energy of your being, and let yourself experience it.

Don't ask yourself, "Am I really experiencing this?" Don't try to second-guess yourself. Accept what comes and *know* that it is a message from the deepest part of yourself. Feel this, savor it. Stay with the feeling as long as you can.

Don't time this exercise. Don't think you must spend, say, fifteen minutes, or half an hour, or any set amount of time on it. This may make it seem like a duty, something to be done whether or not you want to. Above all, this exercise should be an enjoyable one.

It may take a few tries before you recognize that you are in touch with your feeling-tones. Others may have an instant "aha" experience in which you realize you've *always* been in touch with these tones but hadn't taken conscious note of them. In any case, all of you will come to recognize them in time, for they are in no way hidden but are an intimate part of your daily existence. They are your connection with All That Is.

I recommend that you do this exercise often at first—perhaps twice a day—until it becomes second nature. Every now and again, consciously check out your feeling-tones, and when you are upset or depressed, use the sense of power this gives you. When you are consciously aware of your feeling-tones, you feel centered and secure.

To reinforce all this, you might sometimes chant *"O-O-O-O-O-O-M-M-M-M-M-M"* slowly to yourself, either mentally or aloud. This sound is the physical translation of your deep non-physical rhythm, and will tone up your body and energize you. I often use this chant when driving and actually find myself enjoying the traffic.

After you have done this exercise many times and are familiar with the sense of power these feeling-tones give you, sense these tones going outward from your body—for this is exactly what they do. With each breath, with each pulsation of energy, you send out this essence of yourself, which mingles with other essences and creates and re-creates your physical environment. Feel yourself centered within and sending out waves of your energy. See it radiating outward from your physical being and into the environment, where it becomes an extension of yourself. Realize that the objects you perceive "out there" are the materialization of your thoughts, formed by *your* energy into symbols of the inner you, your essence, your soul. Feel that energy radiating down into the center of the earth and up into the sky, past the clouds and into the farthest reaches of the universe, for that is indeed what it does. These emanations from your consciousness do reach outward in this manner, and there is nothing they do not influence.

Such is the nature of your creativity, of your Self.

2

A State
of Becoming

When you say: "I want to find myself," you usually take it for
granted that there is a completed, done, finished version of
yourself that you have mislaid somewhere. When you think of
finding God, you often think in the same terms. Now you are
"around yourself" all the time. You are ever becoming yourself
.... Both God and the psyche are constantly expanding—unuttera-
ble, and always becoming [*The Nature of the Psyche*, p. 108].

The essence of being is action. Our universe—and all others, according to
Seth—is made up of conscious energy, eternally in motion. Every motion of
each bit of energy affects all others, and changes the overall pattern.

Through its motions, each particle of energy distinguishes itself from
the others, and has identity as a separate moving force. Previous to the
Creation, the pool of energy of which we are a part was undifferentiated,
latent, fraught with probabilities, but in a state of nonbeing, of nonaction.
There was Consciousness, but no means of knowing. In order to know what it
was, this energy had to get "outside itself," but once it did this, it changed
from what it was to something else. Then, in order to know what that
something else was, it had to get outside of itself once again.

The act of perceiving something always changes the perceived thing to
something else. Quantum physicists have found this to be the case with small
bits of matter; it is also the case with nonmaterial, psychic energy.

This, then, is Being—a process of becoming what you are, and through
that act of becoming, changing what you are. Were Being ever to be
"finished," it would cease to Be, for it is precisely the process, the motion,
that gives it "life." This process was what All That Is set in motion when It
released a portion of Its energy from its finished, ideal, state to become what
it would become.

Action is the essence of being, and unpredictability is its rule. You
cannot predict with certainty the outcome of any action, since that action
changes the thing it acts upon. In your act of becoming, you change what you
are. And in fact, it is the very unpredictability of action that motivates it. You
would not for long feel curious about the results of any planned action if you
knew for sure that it would turn out a certain way. Precisely because you *don't*

know for sure how it will turn out, you're motivated to take the action necessary to find out. This—your curiosity, your intense desire to know—is what keeps you alive, keeps you becoming.

Considering the dynamic, always-becoming nature of Being, then, it doesn't make sense to speak in terms of "finding" yourself, as if somewhere there were a version of you that exists as a finished product. There *is* an "ideal psychological pattern" (more later), but that pattern can never be realized, since the process of realizing it would automatically change it. So rather than think in terms of "what I'm going to be when I grow up," it's more useful to consider the nature of your becoming. Rather than focus on the product, focus on the process. This way, if not satisfied with your present state of being, you will know what to do about it: change the process, change your actions, and see what effects that procedure has on your state of being: on your state of becoming. One of this workbook's prime objectives is to make you more conscious of what you think and do to create your reality, for only through such awareness can you hope to change aspects you haven't been pleased with.

For this exercise, use your journal. Begin by making a list of things that you have *become* over the years. Think back to periods in your life when you went through noticeable changes from one state of being to another. An obvious example would be a change from dependence on parents to dependence on self. Another would be a change from one emotional state to another. Say you got past depression into a different state of being. Think of several times in your life when you were aware of going through a change, whether for the better or for the worse.

Now try to figure out what you did that was *responsible* for that change. First of all, see if you can pinpoint the *thoughts* you had about your condition prior to changing, and the thoughts you had after the change. No doubt they changed as your state of being did. Now, what did you *do* to bring about this change in your state of being, and in your thoughts? Much of it was probably subconscious, but try to bring to conscious awareness some of the actions you took and emotions you had during the transition period. Did you resist the change, or try to speed it up? Did you change your sleeping or eating habits? Did you make new friends and discard old ones? Did you change your place of residence, your hair style, or your wardrobe? For each period of change, see if you can figure out how you, the creator of that change, brought it about.

Now look for patterns. Do you find that you tended to use the same means for each change (such as changing your eating habits)? Can you find certain strategies that you have used over and over? Have you used certain strategies for changes into what you consider to be a better state of being, and other strategies for changes into less desirable states? Does it seem as if your changes for the better were brought about by you, while the changes for the worse were brought about by "forces beyond your control"? If so, then realize that that is your belief and *thus* your reality, not the other way around.

Now look at your present state of being and see if you can view it as in process. See yourself as having come from one state, and being on the way to another. You are at the halfway point enroute from A to B. From this perspective, view the thoughts and actions that have brought you this far along the route. Now see if you can make any predictions about future thoughts and actions based on the same pattern. What will be the likely results? What state of being will you be in when you reach B?

In your journal, describe the process you are presently in, in as much detail as you can. Are there any aspects to this process you are not satisfied with, which would appear not to be leading to results you want? If so, what process-changes can you make that will have a positive affect on that "product" you are presently becoming? If changes are indicated, promise yourself to take small steps along the way to bring them about.

Now, as a final step in this exercise, envision yourself at the end of this life span. Envision all the *becomings* that you will have experienced by then based on your present patterns of action—while at the same time realizing that the very act of thinking about what you might be going to become will automatically change that product!

3

Framework 1
and Framework 2

As you do not know what happens in the television studio before you observe a program . . . so you do not know what happens in the creative framework of reality before you experience physical events. We will call that vast "unconscious" mental and universal studio Framework 2. . . . It is as if Framework 2 contains an infinite information service, that instantly puts you in contact with whatever knowledge you require, that sets up circuits between you and others, that computes probabilities with blinding speed. Not with the impersonality of a computer, however, but with a loving intent that has your best purposes in mind—yours and also those of each other individual [*The Individual and the Nature of Mass Events*, pp. 81, 83].

To explain the dynamics involved in creating our reality, Seth uses the terms "Framework 1" and "Framework 2" to represent the manifest and unmanifest realities in which we have our experience. Basically, Framework 1 is the physical world, presided over by the ego—that conscious version of ourselves with whom we identify. Framework 2 is the behind-the-scenes reality from which we draw the information involved in the creation of the events we then experience in the physical world. Presiding over this vast "information service" is the inner self—variously called the inner ego, the psyche, the unconscious, the spiritual self, and the soul. This entity selects and interprets the information—in the form of aware-ized energy—coming into it; and sends it on to the ego, who can then choose to act upon it or not.

Seth stresses that this division into frameworks is an arbitrary one, however, made for the convenience of discussion only. In actuality, the two frameworks are complementary and inseparable. Just as our ego depends on the inner self for its manifestation, so too does the inner self constantly seek to become manifest. Both portions are aware of this interdependence, and they meet in intuitions, impulses, dreams, and states of altered consciousness.

Like all creatures of nature, we were born with an impetus toward growth and the development of our capacities—with an impetus toward becoming what we are. And like all creatures of nature, we are mutually dependent on one another in such a way that fulfillment of one leads to the fulfillment of the species. For each of us, then, there is what Seth calls an

16

"ideal psychological pattern." Framework 2—or, rather, the inner self that operates within this framework—is constantly striving to move us in that direction. This pattern is flexible, responding to the changing circumstances of our daily lives, but always moves us in the best possible direction for our own benefit and for the benefit of all that we come in contact with.

Thus, the Framework 2 from which we draw our experience, is not a "neutral" medium at all, but a benevolent one, gently nudging us toward constructive choices. It takes a strong belief in evil to counteract this benevolent force for good. In future exercises we will look at some of the reasons why we mistrust our intuitions and impulses, fear our dreams, and lack confidence in the limitless source of creativity that is at our disposal. You will see that the inner self, unable to experience physical reality directly, depends on the ego to interpret this reality through its beliefs about reality. And then, through its intense desire to see those beliefs made manifest, transforms its energy into physical forms. And we will explore ways of getting in more conscious touch with Framework 2 and the inner self, and of discovering the beliefs we hold that create our reality.

In this exercise, though, we will focus on faith. For underlying much of what we do in Framework 1, is our faith, so much a "given" as to be invisible, that we *can* operate; that Framework 2 will provide us with the knowledge and energy we need to have experiences in Framework 1. We trust, for instance, that the sun will rise in the morning; and so it does. We assume that our stomachs will digest our food; and so they do. We take it for granted when driving a car that, if we turn the steering wheel, the car will go in that direction. And so on—the most minute actions we take are governed by the faith that our intent will be carried through.

Ninety percent of the time we feel no need to weigh the pros and cons before we take some action, for we "know" it will have the results we want. And precisely because we *do* "know" this, precisely *because* we have faith that the desired result will happen, it does.

There is a saying to the effect that you don't have to have faith in something you know. The implication is that knowledge is "rational" while faith is "irrational" (and that knowledge is, somehow, "superior" to faith). But according to Seth, our faith is the source of our knowledge. Since we cannot know the contents of Framework 2 directly, through our normal perceptions, we can proceed only on faith. And insofar as we have faith in something, it manifests. Through these manifestations, we gain knowledge.

So in the Sethian view, faith comes first. Knowledge is the result of faith, not a superior, "rational" state of consciousness. High time, then, that we began having faith in faith instead of distrusting it! As Seth says,

> Faith in a creative, fulfilling, desired end—sustained faith—
> literally draws from Framework 2 all of the necessary ingredients,
> all of the elements however staggering in number, all of the details,
> and then inserts into Framework 1 the impulses, dreams, chance

meetings, motivations, or whatever is necessary so that the desired end then falls into place as a completed pattern [*The God of Jane*, p. 13].

For this exercise, you will create a Credo for yourself, affirming your faith in the workings of Framework 2. Here is one that Robert Butts, Jane Roberts' husband, wrote for himself, which you might want to use as a model:

I have the simple, profound faith that anything I desire in this life can come to me from Framework 2. There are no impediments in Framework 2. Framework 2 can creatively produce everything I desire to have in Framework 1—my excellent health, painting, and writing, my excellent relationship with Jane, Jane's own spontaneous and glowing physical health and creativity, the greater and greater sales of all of her books. I know that all of these positive goals are worked out in Framework 2, regardless of their seeming complexity, and that they can then show themselves in Framework 1. I have the simple, profound faith that everything I desire in life can come to me from the miraculous working of Framework 2. I do not need to be concerned with details of any kind, knowing that Framework 2 possesses the infinite creative capacity to handle and produce everything I can possibly ask of it. My simple, profound faith in the creative goodness of Framework 2 is all that is necessary [*The Individual and The Nature of Mass Events*, p. 84].

Make a poster for yourself, with your Credo written in large black letters, pin it next to your bed or on the bathroom door, and make a point of reading it every time you notice it. Then forget about it, and have the faith that your faith will be rewarded.

4

Here and Now

An animal, not necessarily just a wild one in some native forest, but an ordinary dog or cat, reacts in a certain fashion. It is alert to everything in its environment. A cat does not anticipate danger from a penned dog four blocks away, however, nor bothers wondering what would happen if that dog were to escape and find the cat's cozy yard.

Many people, however, do not pay attention to everything in their environments, but through their beliefs, concentrate *only* upon "the ferocious dog four blocks away." That is, they do not respond to what is physically present or perceivable in either space or time, but instead dwell upon the threats that may or may not exist, ignoring at the same time other pertinent data that are immedately at hand [*The Individual and The Nature of Mass Events*, pp. 49-50].

The physical world is filled with messages. Everything we see "out there"—the wind blowing in the trees, bees buzzing around flowers, the growl of a dog—is there to tell us something. We continually interact with our environment, picking up messages and giving them out. Our body does this automatically, through cellular communication, and in so doing, keeps us functioning safely and effectively. So long as we are alert and tuned in to our physical environment, our minds and bodies work well.

The trouble is, however, that there is also an inner world of concepts, created by the mind, that we have to deal with. The body, through the physical senses, can process information coming in from the biological environment, but to interpret information coming in from the cultural environment, it relies upon the ego. For instance, the body leaves it up to the ego to determine whether a threat is inherent in a particular social situation—and will then act accordingly. Thus, if your next-door neighbor calls you over to the fence with a frown on her face, your body reacts according to the way your mind interprets that frown. If your mind says that the facial expression symbolizes a threat, the body will prepare itself accordingly; if your mind says that no threat is involved, the body goes on functioning as usual.

Now, so long as our mind's assessment of threat correlates with a biological assessment, we and our bodies have a good working relationship, in which the body reacts quickly and appropriately to threat situations. But if we continually perceive dangerous situations for which there are no biological counterparts, such as "the ferocious dog four blocks away," the body has nothing specific to respond to. Yet it *must* respond in some way, and so soon gets overworked and confused. Over time, this can result in illness or some other debilitation, and our natural exuberance and vitality can be lost in the shuffle.

There is of course a reason why the human species has grown so very far apart from nature, why we exploit and try to *control* nature rather than live in harmony with it. The reason has to do with our belief in separation and opposition—perhaps the inevitable outcome of the direction human consciousness has taken on this physical plane. But as Seth says again and again, we cannot appreciate spirituality without appreciating our creaturehood, for the two have much in common. Our body and all of nature are the physical manifestations of the soul. Nature is our inner self talking to us through symbols. On the other hand, the manmade aspects of our reality—including its social and political structure—are manifestations of our ego's beliefs. They are a secondary, less substantial, short-lived manifestation, then; while nature is primary.

This means that when communing with nature, we are a lot closer to our essence than when we're trying to figure out intellectually what really *is* the nature of personal reality (and certainly closer than when we worry about "the ferocious dog four blocks away"!).

Of course, all of this has been said countless times in countless ways. Everyone knows we're too stressed-out. Everyone agrees we worry too much. Everyone admits that if we could just live in the here and now, our bodies would be much better off. Everyone senses that nature is where it's at. Everyone *knows* these things, and one of these days, maybe we'll do something about it. But right now, we're just too busy at work ...

But don't put it off. As Seth says:

> The natural creature-validity of your senses must remain clear, and only then can you take full advantage of those intuitions and visions that must come through your own private intersections with space and time...the ever-actual integrity of nature everywhere surrounds you. It represents your direct experiences. It offers comfort, creativity, and inspiration that you impede only if you allow secondary experience to supersede your daily moment-to-moment encounter with the physical earth [*The Nature of The Psyche*, pp. 213–214].

Do this exercise for five or ten minutes a day. Find a quiet place outdoors where there are some trees and foliage. Sit quietly. Look around you and ask yourself, *What am I conscious of right now?* Take in everything: the colors, the shapes, the textures, the feel of the wind on your face. Vividly experience the scene.

Then close your eyes. Become aware of the many sounds that you may not have noticed before. Identify them, mentally connecting the sound with the object that makes it. Feel your body as part of the natural surroundings. Become aware of its temperature—whether your hands feel warm or cold, or your feet cold and your belly hot. Become aware of the other sensations in your body. Do you have a taste in your mouth? What smells are you conscious of? Sense your connection with nature through smell—smell is both within you and without you, part of you *and* part of nature.

Now open your eyes and bring the inner and the outer together. Feel your connection through the senses with nature. Become aware of the inter-connectedness of all natural phenomena. Feel yourself a part of the process of nature. *Feel* this interaction. Feel all your sensations come together and form a unified whole. Feel your hearing and your vision, your tasting and your smelling, your touch, feel them as *one* unified brilliant perception. Hold the perception in your mind, then close your eyes again. Let this sense of unity fade and sounds become dominant. Follow one particular sound closely, concentrating on it, following it in your mind. Then open your eyes and instantly once again, bring your senses together into a unified whole, all your sensations adding up to a single highly-focused brilliant point of perception.

Let this sense world intensify, then close your eyes and unfocus once more.

After you have done this a few times and are aware of the contrast between perceiving one-thing-at-a-time and a unified whole, you will develop a *feeling* for this unity. You will recognize how you feel when your consciousness is totally in the here and now, focused totally in physical reality.

Every now and again, during your daily routine, try to get this fine focus, with all sense data integrated to provide the most lucid possible perception of physical reality. Over time, you will find that this practice will enrich your daily experience, allowing you to concentrate fully on whatever is genuinely at hand. Your mind and your body will be united to take care of it.

5

Belief Assignment #1

> You form the fabric of your experience through your own beliefs and expectations. These personal ideas about yourself and the nature of reality will affect your thoughts and emotions. You take your beliefs *about* reality as truths and often do not question them. They seem self-explanatory. They appear in your mind as statements of fact, far too obvious for examination.
>
> Therefore they are accepted without question too often. They are not recognized as beliefs *about* reality, but are instead considered as characteristics of reality itself... They become invisible assumptions, but they nevertheless color your experience [*The Nature of Personal Reality*, pp 19-20].

A belief is a thought—with expectations attached.

We are constantly thinking. Each of our thoughts has a reality in Framework 2. Each one is a living entity, a unit of aware-ized energy, rising out of that gestalt of aware-ized energy, the inner self, in the continual interaction of information and knowledge taking place in that framework.

But not all thoughts become materialized in Framework 1. Only those that have sufficient emotional intensity behind them do—thoughts combined with the expectation or desire to manifest. Sometimes, that expectation or desire is based on the ego's assessment of reality—what it expects or wants to see manifested—and sometimes, purely on what the inner self knows to be good for our growth. Whenever an emotion-charged thought comes into awareness, the inner self automatically forms from this inner experience a material counterpart, so that the ego can experience the thought in physical reality. This is happening constantly, with your inner self (and other inner selves) every instant creating and re-creating the material world.

These material counterparts are formed from the energy of the inner self by means of electromagnetic units (EE units, as Seth calls them) which "emanate" from this aware-ized energy (or consciousness) when it is at an emotional pitch. EE units are subatomic particles that make up everything in our physical world—the air, our bodies, rocks, buildings. Through the desire and intent of the inner self, these units emanate outward to form atoms and molecules, cells, and organs, and finally the entire system of camouflage that is our physical reality. What we see "out there" is our inner subjective experience in solidified form—solidified thoughts! Our bodies and every-thing else in our world is organized, built, and maintained by the collective efforts of the inner selves in order to see themselves "objectified" in three-dimensional reality. Such is the power and nature of consciousness.

This, then, is the way reality is created—through expectant thoughts. That is what Seth means when he states, repeatedly, that we create our reality through our beliefs; and that if we want to change our reality, we must first discover the beliefs we have about it. He stresses the fact that these beliefs are *conscious*—not hidden deep somewhere in an inaccessible portion of our mind. But they *may* be invisible to us because we take them to be *facts* about reality rather than beliefs about it.

For example, one belief we all have about reality is that night follows day. And because we all believe this to be the case, it *is* the case. Our belief creates our reality—which means that through contemplating our reality, we can discover our beliefs.

Seth calls beliefs of the kind just mentioned "root assumptions"—ideas upon which we have all agreed to base our existence. All systems of reality (and there is an infinite number of them) have a set of root assumptions that everyone must follow *if* they want to operate within that system. Within our reality, for example, our ideas about time and space are root assumptions. But in other realities, they don't necessarily apply.

Of course, we cannot change our root assumptions and expect to operate within this reality—unless we could somehow get every conscious entity in this reality simultaneously to change to some other agreed-upon assumptions. But each of us holds many other beliefs about this reality that *seem* to be root assumptions. One such belief might be "I am fat." You say to yourself, "The fact that I am fat is a *fact* about reality." However, the fact is, you *believe* you are fat, and so you are. But your *being* fat is not a root assumption about this reality, nor a belief that everyone within this reality has agreed upon as a condition of existence. Whether or not you are fat, this reality will continue to exist, so "I am fat" is a belief that you *can* change. But first you have to thoroughly understand that "I am fat" is really a *belief* and not a fact, and to believe that, you can change that belief and thus your reality.

For several years, Jane Roberts held once-a-week ESP classes which are chronicled in *Conversations with Seth*, by Susan M. Watkins, a friend of Jane's who attended the classes. Seth often made spontaneous "appearances" during these classes, commented on what the students were saying, gave advice, and made assignments for them to do as homework. One set of assignments he gave was "belief papers," in which the students were asked to write about their beliefs in certain areas, then read and discuss their papers at the next class meeting. This workbook will have a similar set of exercises asking you to examine your beliefs in various areas.

For this first exercise, focus on your basic assumptions about *marriage, religion,* and *the role of government.* These are good beliefs to begin with because the assumptions are relatively more visible than they are in less institutionalized areas. In examining your beliefs, begin with the "facts"—for instance, regarding marriage: *Over fifty per cent of the marriages in the U.S. end in divorce*. This is a "fact," or rather a belief that a large number of people ascribe to—but not a root assumption. Now examine the repercussions of this "fact" on your own personal belief system. Do you believe that your own marriage has only a 50% chance of success? Or that these days, a marriage is difficult to maintain? Use "facts," then, to dig into some of your private, personal beliefs.

A second way to discover your beliefs is to examine your *emotions* about the subject. For instance, you may feel angry when you think about the government. What is the belief (or set of beliefs) behind this anger? Our emotions are generated by our beliefs, *not* the other way around—so look to the beliefs that caused the emotion.

Finally, examine your beliefs' effects on your reality. To what actions and experiences do these beliefs lead? Do you like these results? If not, what beliefs would you like to substitute for them? Work on these.

Write about your beliefs in these areas in your journal. If possible, try sharing them with others, for you may find that someone else may not at all agree with what *you* consider to be widely-held "facts". Many of the beliefs that we hold are invisible to us because we take them for granted. ("Everyone knows that.") So include the beliefs that everyone knows, and try them out on others to see if everyone really does.

6

The Point of Power Is Now!

When you rail against an unfavorable environment, or a situation or condition, basically... *you are not acting independently, but almost blindly reacting*...To act in an independent manner, you must begin to initiate action that you want to occur physically by creating it in your own being.

This is done by combining belief, emotion, and imagination, and forming them into a mental picture of the desired physical result. Of course, the wanted result is not yet physical or you would not need to create it, so it does no good to say your physical experience seems to contradict what you are trying to do [*The Nature of Personal Reality*, p. 12].

The Point of Power Is Now! For practical purposes, this is one of the most valuable concepts in the Seth material. It means that we are always in control of our own destiny, for it is *right now*—not in some dim past or unforeseeable future—that our beliefs create our reality. We form our lives from our focal point in the present, at the point where our beliefs intersect with the physical world on the one hand and the unmanifest world (the source of our energy, strength, and inspiration) on the other.

The past and the future are not where the power lies. What we do right here and now in the present constantly influences our past and our future. Time does not exist in Framework 2, and so past and future are happening simultaneously. If we change a belief now, the past *automatically* changes to harmonize with this new belief. And in keeping with this belief future probabilities are altered too.

The past does not determine our present; the present determines our present—*and* our past, and our future. This point cannot be emphasized enough. Whatever we have experienced in the past, whatever our reality was like *one minute* ago, *now* is what forms it now. We are creating ourselves each instant and always have a choice, *now*, of what our reality is like.

If it seems that we are at the mercy of past events over which we have no control, then that is our belief—and that is our reality. But we are not at the mercy of our past, only at the "mercy" of beliefs we either do not recognize or cling to, despite their detrimental effect on our reality. Our beliefs are what form our reality, and *we* are the ones who choose our beliefs. Whatever we believe is faithfully materialized "out there" for us, the creators, to contemplate.

Of course, because of the nature of physical reality, there may be a lag between the time a belief is inserted, and the time of its materialization. For instance, if you change from the "I am fat" belief to the "I am thin" belief, your body will take a while before it reflects this belief back to you. But the instant you insert that new belief from your point of power in the present, your body will begin the changes necessary to bring you into harmony with that belief. And the past will alter too, creating a new past self in tune with the new belief.

All you need do is to believe something, and it will become a part of your reality. This is the main lesson that we are here on earth to learn: that we do create our own reality through our beliefs, *now*.

In the nine belief exercises in this workbook, you will be examining the beliefs you hold very closely—for often they escape your notice because you take them for granted as facts of existence, or they limit you in a way you had not thought about before. Often what you see materialized "out there" will be the result of a cluster of beliefs that need to be revealed before you can change them. It is well worth the work it takes to discover what your beliefs really are, for once you know what they are, you can change them, one by one. You are not powerless to help yourself at all. It just takes discipline and determination and faith in the idea that you are *constantly* creating your own reality through your beliefs, at this very instant.

The Exercise

Sit quietly, and focus all of your energy on the idea that right *now* is the point of power—the eternal instant at which your energy gives form to matter. Feel all of your inner strength, emotions, and intellect intersecting with—and giving life to—your body, to your physical reality. Feel that energy surging through that point of power where the inner world and the outer world meet, going out into the environment and forming your reality. Focus all of your energy on this.

Now, bring into your mind something that you want to see materialized. Feel your whole self responding to this desire—to this belief that you want to experience physically. Feel all of your inner powers working together, intersecting with physical reality at that power point, creating that wanted reality. *Visualize* it happening and *think* about it happening: concentrate on that desire coming to be. Use all your energy and attention to visualize this.

Then forget about it. Once you have imagined your belief coming into being, put it out of your mind. Don't keep looking for the results or checking to see whether it's working. Know that it *is* working; you have put in your request to Framework 2, and waiting is all you have to do. What you have asked for, you *will* receive.

This is another basic exercise that you should do daily. Performed along with the feeling-tones exercise, this should give you a strong sense of the power that is within you; the energy that is yours to use in creating your own reality.

Important! Make sure the new belief is a positive one, e.g., "Pat loves me and wants to be with me," and not "Pat is no longer diffident or aloof." Another thing. Once a day, take some action or make some gesture that's in keeping with the new belief. If you want to get over shyness you might say hello to a stranger, or strike up a conversation with the check-out person in the supermarket. In some way, behave in accordance with your new belief in being comfortable with others. Demonstrate faith in your ability to create your own reality.

At times in your life when for some reason you are feeling powerless— angry, frustrated, or depressed—then use this point of power exercise to get in touch with the energy of your being. A knowledge of your own power automatically frees you of your fears and thus of negative feelings.

All negative feelings are a result of fear, and fear is a result of feeling powerless—helpless before a destiny not your own to shape. As one of Seth's students once remarked, "Evil is inability." "Inability to what?" someone asked, and the answer came back, "Inability, period." Use the point of power exercise every time you are feeling insecure in any way.

7

Dream Play

In a dream, you are basically aware of so many facets of an event that many of them must necessarily escape your waking memory. Yet any real education must take into consideration the learning processes within dreams, and no one can hope to glimpse the nature of the psyche without encouraging dream exploration, recall, and the creative use of dream education in waking life [*The Nature of The Psyche*, p. 166].

In all of Seth's books, dreams play an important part. He considers familiarity with the dream state a necessary prerequisite to understanding the true nature of our reality, and how we create it.

In waking life, our most direct connection with Framework 2 (that inner reality on which our outer reality is based) is limited to impulses, intuitions and hunches—messages sent to our ego by our inner self, operating in Framework 2. Before sending these messages, that suggest actions for us to take, the inner self sorts through the data constantly flowing into it and tries to determine which actions to suggest. One important way to make this determination is via dreams, in which various possibilities are rehearsed and from these, the most productive actions chosen.

In the dream state, the inner self and the outer self—the dreaming ego—meet in a way not possible in waking life, with the inner self observing the dream dramas and the ego participating in them. Through this interaction, the ego gets a firsthand view of how physical reality is created, becomes aware of its ideal psychological pattern, and also experiences the multidimensional world of inner reality—in which we have our after-life existence. For this reason, Seth stresses the importance of becoming *consciously* aware in the dream state. Through bringing this state to conscious awareness, there is much to be learned, for through conscious manipulation of dreams, we can change our physical reality into a more harmonious and fulfilling one.

Repeatedly, Seth suggests that we adopt a sleep pattern that lets the waking mind and the dreaming mind become more aware of one another. The ideal pattern would be to take two three-hour naps during a twenty-four hour period, and certainly to sleep no more than six hours at a time. Anything more than that widens the gap between the dreaming and the waking states and cuts down on mental and physical efficiency. Shortening the sleep time, Seth says, enables the waking self to recall more of the dream adventures.

Another way for us to become more consciously aware of our dream environment is simply to suggest, before going to sleep, that we will "come awake" in our dreams, bring our waking self into the dream and remember the experience. If we use this suggestion repeatedly, night after night, and sincerely want to have this awareness, not harboring any hidden fears about what we might meet in our dreams, eventually we will be able to take the conscious ego into the dream and become aware of depths of experience and knowledge unknown before. This will result in much more flexibility and expanded awareness in waking life.

Dreams are highly creative and playful. Seth likens them to childhood games where children scare themselves on purpose, well aware that it's only a game and that when their mother calls them to dinner, the bogeyman will go away. As we grow older, we learn to feel foolish in pretending, life becomes a *serious* matter, and our playfulness comes out only in the dream state.

Adults' dreams, then, are like child's play. Thus one way for us to discover more about our dreams is to playfully make up dreams for ourselves while in a waking state; to create our own versions of bogeymen and ogres, witches and goblins. This lets us see what symbols are meaningful to us, what situations we set up for ourselves when we dream—for our waking dreams will have much in common with our real ones. This way, we can become aware of the creative flexibility of consciousness that is characteristic of the dreaming state and learn to become more creative and flexible in the waking state as well.

This exercise will focus on a waking dream. It should be done repeatedly. The exercise will work best if you are also recording your nightly dreams at the same time, so that you can compare waking and sleeping dreams. Each night, before going to sleep, suggest to yourself that you will remember your dreams and that you will be consciously aware of them when they are happening. Repeat this suggestion several times, slowly and earnestly; then relax and fall asleep. Keep a notebook and pen next to your bed so that you can write down your dreams as soon as you wake up. But don't just write them down and forget about them. Try to analyze them and see what they are trying to tell you.

Now, in your journal, create a dream for yourself. Do this playfully and without trying to structure what you are writing. Just begin writing and let the images flow without trying to figure out what they mean. Don't try to be logical and stick to one idea. If, in the middle of a sentence, you start going off on another train of thought, let this happen. Try not to put any value judgments on what you're writing ("This is really weird") or lead yourself in a certain direction. Imagine that you are your inner self, watching this dream unfold as you write it down. Imagine, too, that you are the dreaming ego, acting out the events in the dream, playfully, as children do in games. Don't try to put a conclusion on the dream—let it end the way it ends, even if that seems up in the air.

Now try to interpret the dream by playing around with some of the images you came up with. You might want to do some free associations by writing down whatever comes to mind about some of the images. Don't try to force meaning on the dream. Play with it, and see what meaning emerges. The main value of this exercise will be in giving you insights into the nature of your real dreams, and show you what it is like to operate with a more flexible consciousness within a multi-dimensional reality.

Repeat this exercise regularly, and take note of how your made-up dreams change as your reality goes through its characteristic fluctuations.

8

The Role
of Imagination

To understand that you create your own reality requires that same kind of "awakening" from the normal awake state [as one can awaken within a dream and realize he is dreaming]...As long as you believe that either good events or bad ones are meted out by a personified God as the reward or punishment for your actions, or on the other hand that events are largely meaningless, chaotic, subjective knots in the tangled web of an accidental Darwinian world, then you cannot consciously understand your own creativity, or play the role in the universe that you are capable of playing as an individual or as a species. You will instead live in a world where events happen to you in which you must do a sacrifice to the gods of one kind or another, or see yourselves as victims of an uncaring nature.

While still preserving the integrity of physical events as you understand them, you must alter the focus of your attention to some extent, so that you begin to perceive the connections between your subjective reality at any given time, and those events that you perceive at any given time. You are the initiator of those events [*The Individual and The Nature of Mass Events*, pp. 151–2].

As Seth keeps saying, everything in our physical world exists first in our imagination. We tend to think of the physical world as the "real" world, and of the imagination—with its inextricably linked feelings and beliefs—as dreamlike and unreal, or as an offshoot of what happens in the physical world. It just doesn't occur to us that the world we experience might be a *result* of our imaginings, feelings, and beliefs, rather than the other way around. Yet as a matter of fact, our imaginings, feelings, and beliefs are responsible for what happens to us and for how we interpret what happens to us.

This exercise is geared to get you in touch with the "subjective" world of your imagination.

Sit by a window and look out at the world as at a picture. See this picture as the representation of your imaginings, feelings, and beliefs about reality. Sense yourself imagining this picture within, prior to projecting it outward. Feel your inner processes at work, first sketching in a rough outline and then adding to it the details that make this material picture a faithful reproduction of all that you imagine, feel, and believe at this point in time. Feel the power of your energy, as, through desire, it translates this inner reality into a physical picture, so that you can then contemplate and learn from your creation.

Study the details of this picture-through-a-window. What do they say about the inner you? What motivated you to produce just this picture and no other at this particular moment in time? Which aspects of the picture have you perceived differently in different moments? Which aspects always appear the same to you—the same size, shape, color? Which aspects in the picture stand out? Which remain in the background? Why do you think this is the case? What does this say about your beliefs, your feelings, how you conceive of reality?

See if you can change the picture slightly. Playfully direct your imagination to alter the picture in some slight degree, and see the results appear before your eyes. Recognize that it is your imagination, the inner world of your thoughts, feelings, and fantasies, that is creating and altering this picture before you.

It would be a good idea to do this exercise at least once a week until the feeling of creating your own reality is deeply instilled in you. In your journal, keep an account of what happens to you each time you do this exercise—what you discovered about your beliefs, feelings, and fantasies, and what happened when you tried to change them.

9

Impulses:
The Direct Connection

Overall, whether or not you are conscious of it...your lives do
have a certain psychological shape. That shape is formed by your
decisions. You make decisions as the result of feeling impulses to
do this or that, to perform in one manner or another in response to
both private considerations and in regard to demands seemingly
placed upon you by others. In the vast arena of those numberless
probabilities open to you, you do of course have guidelines.
Otherwise you would always be in a state of indecision. Your
personal impulses provide those guidelines by showing you how
best to use probabilities so that you fulfill your own potential to
greatest advantage—and in so doing, provide constructive help to
the society at large.

When you are taught not to trust your impulses, you begin to lose
your powers of decision, and to whatever extent involved in the
circumstances, you begin to lose your sense of power because you
are afraid to act [*The Individual and The Nature of Mass Events*, p.
246].

Our universe is a vast communicative network in which particles of aware-
ized energy constantly in motion are continually exchanging information.
Every particle of energy is conscious of every other particle of energy it comes
in contact with, picking up information from each, and giving it out. Our
body—a gestalt of aware-ized energy—is the same way, constantly giving out
and taking in information.

When we use the term Framework 2 we are referring to this infinite
source of information available to us via aware-ized energy. It is the job of the
inner self to process this information, choosing those bits that are relevant to
the needs, desires, and well-being of the whole self, and sending them on to
the ego, who then decides whether or not to act on these impulses. Impulses,
then, are our direct conscious connection with Framework 2, and provide us
with the impetus toward our ideal pattern of behavior—behavior that will
serve us best at any given point in time.

The trouble is, we have come to distrust our impulses. Because they
arise spontaneously, they seem to us irrational and untrustworthy—something our ego is telling us to do.

We tend to think of ourselves as two distinct entities. First there is the ego, the familiar self that we identify with, who does the acting and the talking, who has a certain personality, feels feelings, and thinks thoughts. Then there is what Seth calls the inner self or psyche, but which we often call the "unconscious" or the soul. To us, it seems remote, mysterious, and unpredictable but nevertheless we look to it for guidance and support in making decisions. We don't trust our familiar everyday self because we have learned that it is wrong to be egotistical, selfish, and aggressive. And so we listen in vain for the "true" inner voice to tell us what to do and how to behave, fearing to take action on the advice of the ego.

The first problem with this attitude comes of thinking of the "conscious" self as the ego, since the term "ego" has, since Freud, taken on a pejorative meaning. Though it still may be defined in the dictionary as "the self or I of any person," most people use the word to connote rash impulsiveness, selfishness, or aggression. Yet there isn't any other agreed-upon word to use instead, so we are stuck with using the word "ego" and, when we do, automatically conjuring up our preconceived ideas about egotistical behavior.

But a more basic problem comes of thinking there are two distinct selves to begin with. As long as we think this way, we will tend to identify with the ego and to separate ourselves from the "unconscious" self. Because of this sense of separation, we won't recognize the messages we are getting as coming from the inner self but instead ascribe them to the ego and therefore regard them as untrustworthy. Thus we fail to recognize how intimately connected we are with the so-called "unconscious"—but in truth, as Seth points out, *more* conscious—self. We fail to recognize that our familiar everyday self with which we are so intimate is the *sum total* of all different parts of ourself working together in order to express *us/me/you* in the flesh. The inner self is not hidden from us, but simply invisible because we have chosen to think that it is something remote and "up there" as opposed to the ever-recognizable ego.

The interesting thing is, we don't think of *other* people as being just an ego. When we look at someone, we realize we are viewing a whole being whose inner self clearly expresses itself through the light in the eyes, a fleeting smile, a tone of voice, each small gesture. It never enters our mind that this is just an ego we are viewing; we *know* better than that. And yet we tend to view ourselves that way—which leads us to distrust our impulses, to a feeling they will get us into trouble.

It is not our impulses that are ego-generated, however, but the *actions* that we choose to take or not in response to the impulses. The ego is the recipient of the impulses, not the originator of them. It is not up to the ego to pass on impulses to "us"—whatever "us" means in that context—but rather to make a decision, based on the beliefs it has to work with, whether or not to take action. And all too often, because of this distrust of impulses, it chooses not to.

As Seth emphasizes repeatedly, impulses are inherently good, coming as they do from Framework 2 which contains our ideal psychological pattern, our blueprint for constructive action. Framework 2 is the creative construct from which comes the knowledge of what is in our best interests and in the best interests of the world, and our impulses are our direct connection with this source of wisdom. They are meant to keep us healthy biologically and psychologically. So it isn't following our impulses that gets us in trouble, but denying them. When we deny our impulses repeatedly, when we do not express them directly, they will find other ways to express themselves and make their messages known to us. Jane Roberts talks about this in *Mass Events:*

> I've had my own hassles with impulses, following only those I thought would lead me where I wanted to go, and drastically cutting down those I feared might distract me from my work. Like many other people, I thought that following my impulses was the least dependable way of achieving any goal—unless I was writing, when impulses of a "creative" kind were most acceptable. I didn't realize that all impulses were creative. As a result of such beliefs, I've had a most annoying arthritis-like condition for some years that was, among other things, the result of cutting down impulses toward physical motion [p. 8].

In Jane's case, the denied impulses expressed themselves through her body, through physical symptoms. Since she denied impulses that were trying to give her the message that her body needed exercise, the inner self came up with the same message in a different form. For others, denied impulses may express themselves psychologically through depression, frustration, or anger.

Generally, it is more difficult to recognize the message behind psychological symptoms than it is physical ones. For example, we tend to view an impulse toward anger as proof that we cannot trust our impulses rather than to interpret the anger as the sign of a denied impulse, an impulse toward some constructive action. And so, rather than trying to discover the source of the anger, we deny that secondary impulse as we did the primary one that led to it—either by failing to recognize the anger to begin with or by pretending that we aren't angry—and thus create more symptoms. The more we deny our impulses, the more powerless we feel, and the more powerless we feel, the more intense the impulse to act—to take action of any kind in order to relieve the pressure. Violent crimes are one of the common results.

Violence, then, is *not* a result of obeying our deepest natural impulses, but rather a result of repeatedly denying those impulses to the point where any action—even action which is far from ideal—is preferable. Our original impulses are benevolent, impelling us toward the best possible development of our capacities. But if we choose not to follow them, we will *still* develop—one way or the other, for this is a dynamic universe and nothing is static. If we don't heed the messages given us at first, in the most positive possible way, then more messages will follow, continuing inexorably until we are finally forced to take action. At that point, we may not even feel that we have a choice whether or not to take action, which only adds to our sense of powerlessness and being at the mercy of a hostile universe.

So we need to recognize and trust our natural impulses, which put us in touch with the power and wisdom to take positive action, meaningful action that achieves good results. The exercise that follows, designed to help you do this, is in two parts. The first part is concerned with recognizing impulses, and the second is concerned with examining what you consider to be negative or destructive impulses.

Part One

For this, use a small notebook, one you can stick in a pocket or purse and have with you at all times. Simply make a note of every impulse you become aware of, no matter how miniscule or silly it seems, no matter whether or not you follow through on it, or whether it seems constructive or destructive. Note the location, the date, and the approximate time you recognized the impulse, and write a short phrase to describe it and what, if anything, you did about it. For example: "Supermarket, 5/15, 3:30. Thought of buying a greeting card for Jan—haven't heard from her in a long time. Looked through rack. Nothing right. Didn't get."

In this exercise, it isn't important whether the impulse is a primary one—a call to positive action, or whether it is a secondary one, arising out of a denied primary impulse. The important thing here is to note down as many instances as possible in which you have become aware of your impulses. The decision simply to write them down will automatically bring to conscious awareness many impulses that you had not thought about before, even if you took action as a result of them.

If you keep this up and periodically review what you've done, you will find that a pattern will emerge. Some impulses may be easy to describe, and other ones won't—you'll be aware of an impulse, of an inner urge to act, but you might not be quite sure what that action is supposed to be. This would indicate an area in which you are less trusting of your inner wisdom.

You may be able to categorize the impulses into such areas as "work", "friends" and "health" and from this, get an idea about how freely you are acting in each area. Or you may categorize them as emotional impulses—anger, frustration, desire, etc.—and physical impulses—to buy something, to write a letter, to get some exercise—or perhaps as primary and secondary impulses. In any case, simply by faithfully recording every impulse you notice over a period of time, you will become increasingly aware of your intimate connection with Framework 2, and realize you are getting your information and messages from it. No longer will you feel cut off from this source of wisdom. You will also see where and how you are blocking impulses, and will gradually learn to take small positive steps here and now rather than wait until you are pushed into drastic action out of the pent-up pressure of denied impulses. Whether or not you decide to follow your impulses, the decision will have been a conscious one rather than an unconscious one.

This method of jotting down impulses can also be used successfully by people who want to get rid of what they consider to be bad habits. I had a friend who was smoking two packs of cigarettes a day and didn't enjoy it, but couldn't seem to stop or even cut down. Often she'd find herself with a cigarette in her mouth without remembering having lit it. She tucked a note card and a stub of a pencil into her cigarette pack, and every time she felt the impulse to smoke, she'd make a tally mark on the card and after that, decide whether or not to follow through on the impulse. Just by bringing these impulses to full conscious notice she was able to cut down her smoking to one pack a day within a week. Not only that, she began to see a pattern in her smoking habit, and to see that smoking was a way to ease (but also perpetuate) a number of small frustrations over which she didn't think she had any control. She subsequently took steps to relieve some of those frustrations and came to feel much better about herself.

Part Two

In the first part of this exercise you were noting down the small everyday repetitive impulses—primary or secondary—that tend to escape notice because, taken singly, they seem to have very little effect on us one way or the other. And in looking them over, you may have found that, cumulatively, some of them *did* have an effect, either positive or negative from your viewpoint.

For this part I would like you to choose impulses to work on which, because of their strength and the feeling of pressure behind them, you recognize to be secondary impulses, resulting from the denial of the gentler primary impulses. A feeling of anger or frustration, a strong desire to overeat or drink, or a drive to prove to someone you are right about something are just a few examples.

Try to recall a recent incident in which you felt a strong impulse. Relive that incident in your mind in every detail. Then write about it in your journal, as if you were writing up a case study from the viewpoint of an observer. What led up to the incident? Were there other incidents like it in the past? What led up to those? What do the incidents have in common? Taking for granted that your strong feelings were motivated out of a sense of powerlessness, see if you can discover what it is that you felt powerless about. You felt prevented from taking some positive, beneficial action; and so you felt powerless. What was that positive beneficial action? Perhaps you wanted to help someone but someone or something seemed to stand in the way. What? Perhaps you had a creative idea but were prevented from expressing it. What was the idea, and how might you express it?

Every time you have a troublesome impulse—one that seems to go in contradiction to what you believe is right or good or true—examine it in this way. You will soon find that it arose after a long process of repressing impulses toward some ideal action—perhaps an action you felt too impossibly idealistic to ever achieve. Plan to take small steps toward achieving that ideal. As you come to trust your primary impulses and take steps to follow through on them, you will gain an ever-increasing sense of power and connection with your inner self and Framework 2.

10

Belief Assignment #2

When you find these thoughts in yourself you may say, and rather indignantly: "But those things are all true. I am poor. I cannot meet my bills," and so forth. In so doing, you see, you accept your belief about reality as a characteristic of reality itself, and so the belief is transparent or invisible to you. But it causes your physical experience... You may follow your thoughts in another area, and find yourself thinking that you are having difficulty because you are too sensitive. Finding the thoughts you may say, "But it is true; I am. I react with such great emotion to small things." But it is a belief, and a limiting one.

If you follow your thoughts further you may find yourself thinking, "I am proud of my sensitivity. It sets me apart from the mob," or "I am too good for this world." These are limiting beliefs [*The Nature of Personal Reality*, p. 45].

As Seth says, many of our beliefs limit our activities and restrict us from expressing ourselves. First of all, we need to find out what the beliefs are (for many of them are invisible) and second to see their limitations clearly. Once we understand how we limit ourselves, then we will be motivated to change our limiting beliefs.

In going through these belief assignments, it is important to have a playful attitude. Instead of regarding limiting beliefs as heavy obstacles that keep you from accomplishing what you wish to, think of them as children's building blocks that you can move around at will. If you put together a structure you don't like, you can always knock it down and start anew.

For this belief exercise, begin with this list of limiting beliefs, compiled from the Seth books and other sources. As you go down the list, check those beliefs that you *feel* to be true—even if, intellectually, you "know" better—and/or which you cannot see the limitations to. Often the limiting beliefs most difficult to spot are those you consider to be "good." In your journal, examine each of these beliefs at length to discover other beliefs which might be behind them, as in the example Seth gives of someone who believes himself to be sensitive, and finds that he is proud of it because it sets himself apart from the mob. What results do these beliefs have? Do you feel limited by them? If so, why are you limiting yourself through these beliefs? What can you do to change them?

1. Women have a hard lot in life.

2. When you're over thirty (forty, fifty, etc.), it's all down hill.

3. It is not all right to show anger.

4. I am a bore.

5. Life is a valley of sorrows.

6. The body is inferior.

7. I am helpless before circumstances that I cannot control.

8. I am helpless because my personality and character were formed in infancy, and I am at the mercy of my past.

9. I am helpless because I am at the mercy of events from past lives in other reincarnations, over which now I have no control. I must be punished or I am punishing myself for unkindnesses done to others in past lives. I must accept the negative aspects of my life because of my karma.

10. I can't help how I feel (or what I think, or do, or believe).

11. People are basically bad, and out to get me.

12. I have the truth and no one else has. Or, my group has the truth and no other group has.

13. I am better (worse) than so-and-so.

14. My existence is dependent upon my experience in flesh. When my body dies, my consciousness dies with it.

15. I am sickly and always have been.

16. There is something wrong with money. People who have it are greedy, less spiritual than those who are poor. They are unhappier, and snobs.

17. I never have enough money.

18. I am not creative. I have no imagination.

19. People dislike me.

20. I can never do what I want to do.

21. I am fat/shy/lazy, etc. or So-and-so is fat/shy/lazy, etc.

22. I always have bad luck.

23. I am dumb.

24. Nobody loves me.

25. I am not a good mother/father.

26. Motherhood (or money, or being beautiful, talented, etc.) is the most important thing in life.

27. I hate violence.

28. I am tired at night.

29. Smoking causes cancer.

30. If I keep drinking as much as I have been, I'll become an alcoholic.

31. I talk too much.

32. I am not musically inclined.

33. I was born with a violent temper.

34. I never got any love, so how can I give it?

35. People are basically hostile.

36. I am too sensitive.

37. It is dangerous to go places alone at night.

38. _____is a ripoff. _____always rip you off.

39. I am frightened of dreams. My bad ones so often come true.

40. Life is meaningless.

41. Wealth is everything.

42. I feel guilty when _____or, I am _____because I feel guilty.

43. I just cannot communicate with so-and-so.

44. I am at the mercy of unconscious drives over which I have no control.

45. I cannot stop smoking (overeating, etc.) because I have no will power.

46. Consciously I want to remember my dreams, but suggestions do not work. Therefore, what I want on a conscious level has little significance.

47. I am too old (young, shy, etc.) to _____.

48. I am lonely. I can't help being lonely.

49. It is too late in life to change my behavior.

50. I think too much. I should be more involved in sports (more outgoing, etc.).

51. I am too weak to resist.

52. I will think only good thoughts and therefore be healthy, and inhibit my bad thoughts and do anything at all with them but think them.

53. Sexual thoughts are bad.

54. I am unworthy; I have no right to happiness.

55. Aggression is bad.

56. I feel inferior.

57. Women are relatively powerless without a man.

58. I am a failure.

59. Age is meaningless to me.

60. I am a writer/artist/doctor/teacher, etc.

61. I have to justify my existence.

62. Idleness is bad.

63. You are what you eat.

64. You'd better buy health insurance.

65. Only a doctor can cure me.

66. I need a lot of sleep.

67. I am superior to others because of my talent.

68. I have no control over what happens to me.

69. I am super-responsible

70. Sensory perception is the only source of knowledge or truth

71. Women are feminine; men are masculine.

72. More is better.

73. All science is certain evident knowledge.

74. Mind over matter.

75. All aspects of complex phenomena can be understood by reducing them to their constituent parts.

76. We are isolated egos existing "inside" our bodies.

77. Mental labor is superior to manual labor.

78. We "own" our body.

79. There is no purpose, life, or spirituality in matter.

80. Nature is a machine; the body is a machine.

81. The aim of science is the domination and control of nature.

82. Disease is a malfunction of a specific biological mechanism; a doctor's job is to repair that part of the machine.

83. Health is the absence of disease.

84. Anything that alleviates pain temporarily is necessarily good.

85. At birth, the mind is a blank slate upon which ideas are imprinted by sensory impressions.

86. Thinking and emotions are modes of behavior in response to exterior stimuli.

87. Hard, self-denying work, and worldly success equal virtue.

88. Continual economical and technological growth are essential and good.

89. The Russians (Chinese, etc.) are our enemies.

11

Guilt and Grace

Guilt is the other side of compassion. Its original purpose was to enable you to empathize on an aware level with yourselves and other members of creaturehood, so that you could consciously control what was previously handled on a biological level alone. Guilt in that respect therefore has a strong natural basis and where it is perverted, misused, or misunderstood, it has that great terrifying energy of any runaway basic phenomenon [*The Nature of Personal Reality*, p. 164].

Guilt pervades our culture, though for the most part it is unnecessary and destructive. We feel guilty about eating junk food, guilty for sleeping late on Saturday mornings; we feel guilty when we see a policeman, we feel guilty for saying "no," for saying "yes." ... The list goes on and on. The amount of energy we expend on guilt over imagined wrongdoings is astronomical. Guilt erodes our self-esteem, interferes with our daily functioning, even causes illness and severe depression. And most of the time, there is no logical reason for it. We haven't violated any moral or ethical codes, we haven't done anything to harm another, in some cases we haven't done anything at all—and *that* makes us feel guilty. How did this mass phenomenon come about?

Seth explains that guilt arose as a necessary substitute for the animal instincts that man lost as he evolved into a new state of consciousness. Before that time he existed like all other natural creatures, in a constant state of grace. This state of being rises out of being perfectly attuned to nature, growing effortlessly, joyfully accepting all that life brings, taking for granted the satisfaction of daily needs, living fully in the eternal now. Animals have an instinctive sense of the unity and interdependence of all nature, a biological sense of integrity and empathy, which automatically regulates their behavior.

Man is the first earthly creature to have evolved in consciousness past this instinctive state of being. His impetus toward the development of free will necessitated that he break out of the self-regulated, limiting reign of nature in order to choose for himself the values he would live under. The built-in rules that maintained the equilibrium of nature became guidelines for him rather than hard and fast laws, and conscious compassion replaced the biological imperative against violation of others. This meant that man was free to experiment with his actions, but also responsible for them, for he was aware of their effect on other creatures. Thus guilt was born—natural guilt as

Seth calls it, for it arose out of a need to regulate on a conscious level what had been instinctively regulated on a biological level before. It was an evolutionary step, essential to maintain the balance of nature with its inbuilt sense of justice.

Natural guilt was preventative rather than punitive, in that whenever man violated nature in some way, his feeling of guilt would deter him from taking the same action in the future. The only "punishment" involved was in his resulting sense of guilt, which temporarily dominated the consciousness and cut him off from the feeling of grace that he was still intimately connected to. When he felt guilty, he lost the great joyous sense of support that still characterized his existence.

Man's consciousness of past, present, and future (an awareness few animals have developed to any degree) was closely allied to this sense of natural guilt, and it may be that the guilt concept served as a tool in deepening time-consciousness in man. For guilt depended upon an awareness in the present of past actions and upon the projection into the future of proposed actions. The more man reflected, the more adroit he became at manipulating these concepts in his mind.

Unfortunately for us, however, a deepening of the time sense gradually led, in turn, to a broadening of the guilt sense. Guilt came to be used less as a safeguard against the violation of natural laws and more as a means for one person or faction to foist arbitrary values on others. As artificial guilt and conscience superseded natural guilt and compassion, man increasingly lost sight of his birthright, of his inviolable position in the scheme of things, and came to regard himself as a flawed creature whose existence on earth was suspect and in need of constant justification. Pride didn't go before the fall at all; the fall separated man from his pride.

This exercise will be in two parts, the first concerned with guilt, and the second with grace.

Part One

In your journal, make a list of all the things you can think of that make you feel guilty. Leave some blank spaces between each item on the list, to be filled in later. Here are some questions that will get you thinking about your areas of guilt.

- What actions have you taken that you have felt guilty about?
- What feelings have you had that you thought you shouldn't have and thus felt guilty about?
- What guilt feelings do you have as a result of your relationship with your parents?
- with your body?
- with sex?

- with your peers?
- with your mate?
- with your children?
- with your boss?
- with your co-workers?
- with your church?
- with your government?
- with society?
- with the world?
- with animals?
- with money?
- with property?
- with duties, chores, and rituals?

Now look over your list and put N in front of those items you believe to be examples of natural guilt—guilt arising out of a violation of natural law (necessary to maintain the balance of nature), and put A in front of those you believe to be examples of artificial guilt—arising out of a violation of arbitrary manmade values.

Now examine the beliefs behind each of your examples—both the N's and the A's. For instance, if you said that you felt guilty about spending money on clothes for yourself, *why* do you think it is wrong to do this? Is it because you believe you don't deserve to have new clothes? Because you believe the money should be used for other things, or that you can't afford it? Write the beliefs below the examples they go with.

See if you want to change some of the N's to A's, or vice versa. Did this change your perspective on natural and artificial guilt?

Now on a separate page in your journal examine your beliefs about guilt in general. If you did not believe in guilt, you would not of course have the guilt feelings that you have just discussed. So what are your beliefs about guilt? Is it necessary to feel guilty? What do you get out of feeling guilty? What would happen if you didn't believe in guilt? What would happen if other people didn't believe in guilt? Who needs guilt?

Part Two _____

When we feel guilty, we are not able to experience the state of grace that is our natural heritage. When we experience grace, we cannot experience guilt. Hence one way of getting over a guilt feeling is to get back in touch with that sense of grace.

We experience a state of grace when we sense our deep feeling-tones, for they put us in touch with the nature of our being, our natural exuberance, our importance and worth as human beings. So, continue doing the exercise on feeling-tones regularly, and as you do so, envision your rightness in the world, the effortlessness with which you continue creating yourself with each moment point. Savor the sense of perfect attunement that you feel. This is your state of grace.

12

Opposites:
A Human Construct

...Opposites have a validity only in your own system of reality ... Your conception of good and evil results in large part from the kind of consciousness you have presently adopted....Since you must operate within the world *as* you perceive it, then the opposites will appear to be conditions of existence. These elements have been isolated for a certain reason, however. You are being taught, and you are teaching yourselves to handle energy, to become conscious cocreators with All That Is, and one of the "stages of development" or learning processes includes dealing with opposites as realities.

In your terms, the ideals of good and evil help you recognize the sacredness of existence, the responsibility of consciousness. The ideas of opposites also are necessary guidelines for the developing ego. The inner self knows quite well the unity that exists [*Seth Speaks*, pp. 387–8].

It all started with a disobedient act. One day, Eve was wandering around the Garden of Eden and spotted a beautiful red apple hanging from a branch of the Tree of Knowledge just within her reach. She knew she wasn't supposed to eat fruit from that tree, but on impulse—following some voice within—she took a bite of it. And instantly a new species of consciousness was born. A consciousness separated from nature and instinct, whose deepest beliefs from that time on would be based on opposites, reflecting this sense of separation and alienation.

(As an aside, I'd like to say that Eve has had nothing but bad reviews for this act, which some people think has caused nothing but trouble. But I think she deserves an award for her courage and faith in impulsively taking an unprecedented action. It isn't *her* fault that we're having a hard time dealing with the responsibility that this new kind of consciousness entails. She did more than her share in taking it on to begin with, and thus giving us an unprecedented opportunity for growth and fulfillment on a level that the animals in their limited paradise can't possibly imagine ... But now back to the problems this has caused us.)

Myths are highly-distilled truths, of course, and it actually took a long time for man to become as alienated from nature as he now is. Still, it really did all start with *one* act. Someone had an impulse to do something—his or her inner self, always with the ideal development of the whole self as a goal, was urging the ego to take a small step in the direction of growth in consciousness. This someone heeded that voice, and for the first time in the history of the species, a freely-willed action was taken.

Now before this time, man, like all other natural creatures, had no need for memory. It was not necessary to remember things when everyone was automatically doing what nature prescribed, but it became necessary once the unexpected happened. It may be that the astonishingly unexpected nature of the first act of free will impressed it on the mind and made it memorable, but in any case, once that act was performed, memory became necessary. Otherwise, free will would never have worked. Memory, then, developed apace with these independent acts, which probably gained in popularity very quickly. This led to the development of natural guilt. As we have seen, since the species had compassion for other natural creatures, it did not make them feel good if they harmed or violated another. When this happened, they momentarily lost their sense of exuberance about life, their sense of grace— and this they remembered. The next time the opportunity to perform the same act came around, they conjured up how they had felt in the past, projected into the future how they would feel if they did it again, and decided *not* to do it.

This, then, was natural guilt, triggered by compassion, and made possible by memory. There was nothing punitive about it, other than the temporary loss of *joie de vivre* experienced when doing something that didn't turn out well. But mainly it served as a deterrent. The species was learning, on a conscious level, what the instinct had told them before: *thou shalt not violate.*

As man developed his ability to reflect about the past and to project into the future (a development enhanced by natural guilt) and as he was able to contain more images in his mind, it became necessary to make distinctions among the various images—otherwise, they would all blur together. Some of his remembered past experiences he found more pleasant to recall than others, and this distinction between pleasant and not-so-pleasant was useful in keeping the different images in his mind separate from one another. But it eventually polarized into the good-evil dichotomy so deeply rooted in our consciousness today.

In the meantime, this distinction-making propensity, like natural guilt, served to further develop the human mind. Soon the species were educating their young, passing on knowledge that the elders had picked up. The new species still had a strong survival instinct, and the early education attempts were largely survival-oriented. When the elders recounted their past experiences, they would tend to emphasize the ones that had had negative results, so that children would learn not to make the same mistakes. Because these messages were concerned with survival, they tended to have a heavy emotional load. The children learned to associate negative emotions with disease and death and predators. In doing so, they began to lose the overall view they had once had, in which health and disease, life and death were seen as aspects of a unified whole.

Then the species discovered value judgments. Now, with natural guilt, there had been no judgment involved. If a person did something that she recognized was a violation, she felt guilty, remembered that feeling and didn't do it again. But no one condemned her for what she had done. After all, how could she have known it would be a violation until she directly experienced it and felt the guilt? But as the species began to learn through second-hand experience, the situation changed. Children were told that to do a certain thing would lead to unpleasant consequences. They were not expected to experience this to find out it was true. Thus, if someone went ahead and did something anyway, after being told the consequences, it was considered "bad." The act was bad; thus *he* was bad.

Once the species started using value judgments, there was no end to them. A person could be judged bad for doing something even if he hadn't been told it was taboo. Or he could be bad because he accidentally did something. Or he could be bad for *thinking* something. In this context, natural guilt became all but meaningless, while artificial guilt assumed vast proportions. Compassion—the voice of nature—was scarcely heard over the ever-more demanding voice of society, Conscience.

Artificial guilt, then, arose out of value judgments, and the making of value judgments was an inevitable consequence of distinctions man used to aid his memory. At first these distinctions were subtle ones—pleasant/not so pleasant, say—but then they became polarized either/or, black/white distinctions—so that if something was not "pleasant," it *had to be* "unpleasant." The similarities and connections between two events (and later, objects and concepts) were ignored and their differences emphasized so that they were seen as diametric opposites.

We believed in this opposition, and so it became a reality in our system. But, as Seth says, it is *not* a reality in other systems where the concepts of time and space don't operate, where everything is perceived at once and so there is no need for holding distinctions in the memory. Because we perceive experience in bits, one after another, we can make distinctions that in other systems would be impossible. But if we can realize that these are arbitrary distinctions, highly creative constructs rather than facts about reality itself, we would be less locked in to seeing the world in terms of dichotomies and making judgments accordingly.

For instance, one dichotomy we have created is sickness/health. You're *either* sick *or* you're not sick; it is difficult for us to conceive of something in between. Then we go on to judge sickness as bad and health as good. People who get sick, then, feel guilty. They are bad because sickness is bad.

As Seth says, illness and health are a matter of balance in the body. What we perceive as illness is a sign that the body is out of balance and is automatically taking steps to correct it. This is a natural process, occurring in cycles. Each person has a different pattern. From this perspective, illness and disease are therapeutic, intended to maintain the body's stability. The animals understand this instinctively. But we have lost this instinctive understanding and have come to fear illness, and see it as totally destructive. And so destruction through illness often comes about.

Of course, the basic dichotomy in our reality—the one underlying all others—is the good/evil distinction. We fervently believe in the existence of evil, and so it exists in our reality. It is almost impossible for us to conceive of a world in which evil does not exist, since we see it around us all the time—as a faithful reflection of our beliefs. It seems to us to be a basic property of our reality, like space and time—a root assumption. But it is not a *necessary* belief. While we cannot function in this reality without believing in space and time, we *can* function without believing in evil. Seth says about this:

> While this may seem like the sheerest Pollyanna, nevertheless, *there is no evil in basic terms.* This does not mean that you do not meet with effects that appear evil, but as you move individually through the dimensions of your own consciousness, you will understand that all seeming opposites are other faces of the one supreme drive toward creativity [*The Nature of Personal Reality,* p. 283].

If we can come to view what we have previously labelled "evil" or "bad" as *creative* acts, and realize that we are all here on this plane to learn the responsibility of consciousness and the sacredness of life; if we can view evil as a lesson in "what not to do next time"; if we can trust the sense of natural guilt and compassion to guide us and others and not get caught up in fear and blaming, then evil would lose its power and eventually its reality in our system.

The exercise that follows is a long one, in two parts. You might want to do it in two sessions.

Part One

The concept of opposites, as we have seen, grew out of the necessity to make choices from among possible actions, and thus to distinguish one action from another. At first these distinctions were subtle ones, but later they became polarized into either/or, black/white distinctions. This quite naturally led to the making of value judgments. In this exercise, you are going to take a look at the distinctions you make, and the judgments you form about varrious qualities.

What are your value judgments of the following attributes? Go down the list *quickly*—don't second-guess—and check whether you feel positive (Pos), negative (Neg), or neutral (Neut) about each trait.

Trait	Pos.	Neg.	Neut.
1. active			
2. afraid			
3. aggressive			
4. angelic			
5. angry			
6. anxious			
7. altruistic			
8. argumentative			
9. assertive			
10. athletic			
11. attractive			
12. austere			
13. beautiful			
14. blind			
15. bold			
16. boyish			
17. brave			
18. bright			
19. calculating			
20. calm			
21. carefree			
22. careful			
23. casual			
24. cautious			
25. charming			
26. clear			
27. clever			
28. closed			
29. cold			
30. colorful			
31. cool			
32. compassionate			
33. competitive			
34. conscious			
35. conservative			
36. cooperative			

Trait	Pos.	Neg.	Neut.
37. creative			
38. critical			
39. cunning			
40. daring			
41. dark			
42. dedicated			
43. dependent			
44. depressed			
45. devoted			
46. dirty			
47. disciplined			
48. diseased			
49. domestic			
50. eager			
51. earthy			
52. eccentric			
53. emotional			
54. energetic			
55. even-tempered			
56. exotic			
57. fancy			
58. fast			
59. fat			
60. fearful			
61. feminine			
62. firm			
63. flexible			
64. forceful			
65. foreign			
66. formal			
67. frank			
68. frightened			
69. frightening			
70. frugal			
71. girlish			
72. handsome			
73. happy			

Trait	Pos.	Neg.	Neut.
74. healthy			
75. high			
76. honest			
77. hostile			
78. hot			
79. idealistic			
80. imaginative			
81. impartial			
82. impish			
83. impulsive			
84. independent			
85. inspiring			
86. instructive			
87. intelligent			
88. intense			
89. intuitive			
90. inventive			
91. irreligious			
92. irresponsible			
93. liberal			
94. light			
95. low			
96. manmade			
97. masculine			
98. maternal			
99. mercurial			
100. meticulous			
101. modest			
102. moral			
103. natural			
104. needy			
105. nonathletic			
106. noisy			
107. nurturing			
108. old			
109. open			
110. optimistic			

Trait	Pos.	Neg.	Neut.
111. parental			
112. particular			
113. passionate			
114. paternal			
115. peaceful			
116. permissive			
117. persistent			
118. persuasive			
119. physical			
120. plain			
121. polite			
122. poor			
123. powerful			
124. practical			
125. predictable			
126. protective			
127. psychic			
128. quick-tempered			
129. quiet			
130. rash			
131. rational			
132. realistic			
133. religious			
134. responsible			
135. rich			
136. risky			
137. risk-taking			
138. romantic			
139. rough			
140. sad			
141. scientific			
142. seductive			
143. self-contained			
144. sensitive			
145. sensual			
146. serious			
147. sexy			

Trait	Pos.	Neg.	Neut.
148. short			
149. shy			
150. silent			
151. simple			
152. sloppy			
153. slow			
154. smooth			
155. sophisticated			
156. sour			
157. spiritual			
158. spontaneous			
159. stoical			
160. strict			
161. strong			
162. stylish			
163. subtle			
164. sultry			
165. supportive			
166. sweet			
167. talkative			
168. tall			
169. thin			
170. thrifty			
171. timid			
172. tolerant			
173. truthful			
174. ugly			
175. unassuming			
176. unconscious			
177. unpredictable			
178. uplifting			
179. warm			
180. weak			
181. wise			
182. young			

Now check the *five* traits you feel most strongly positive about, and the *five* traits you feel most strongly negative about. In your journal write: To be *(fill in the trait)* is to .... Then let your images flow. This will reveal your beliefs about the reality concerning that trait. Do the same for the other traits you have chosen.

Part Two

From the list of traits, find *opposing pairs* that you marked positive/negative. For instance, one opposing pair is old/young. If you have marked one of these positive and the other negative, then use it here. For each pair, write down in your journal everything the two traits have *in common*, and the *connections* between them. Begin by examining your beliefs about the traits if you haven't already, and then see what these beliefs—both the positive and the negative ones—have in common. Using the old/young distinction as an example, perhaps you believe that "old" is incapacitating, and "young" is carefree. From this, then you might make the connection that "not having the capacity to take care of yourself" is what makes the young carefree, and that this might well apply to the old as well.

13

A Dialogue

Dialogues is now a book, just completed, but it also represented a movement of the self through a question-and-answer format, through which Ruburt [Jane Roberts] recognized and faced many diverse beliefs. Each reader can utilize the same method whether or not artistic achievement is involved, through objectifying personal beliefs in a dialogue form. This also happens frequently in the dream state, when you allow your natural creativity so much freedom. Often there are dreams in which "you" are two separate people, either strangers or familiar, each asking questions of the other [*The Nature of Personal Reality,* p. 259].

The book Seth is referring to in the quotation is *Dialogues of the Soul and Mortal Self in Time,* a volume of poetry in which Jane Roberts portrays a dialogue between mind and body—two seemingly opposing sides of her self. In the Preface, she tells how she came to write the book:

... *Dialogues* was triggered almost comically by a trivial enough event. A well-known writer referred to me in a national magazine as middle-aged. His article mentioned my books and ideas, in which all time is seen as simultaneous, and my work was treated quite fairly. But I felt humiliated and furious, and no matter what I told myself intellectually, I couldn't shake the emotional outrage.

I found myself in tears, shouting and swearing vigorously. At the same time I saw the humor in the situation, but this only angered me further. I refused to deny the validity of my emotions, so I went along with them. Yet I was struck by the difference between my intellectual concepts about time and my emotional reaction to it, at least in this instance. The mind haughtily went its way, while the body was faced with its daily encounter with time and the seasons. And here "I" was, caught in this gap of understanding, suspended between mind and body's experience of reality. But "I" was hot, angry, stuffy from crying; so there, anyhow, emotions and corporal sensations held sway.

And how could you reconcile the two? I stood there, blowing my nose, quite clearly aware of three separate lines of awareness: emotional uprushes of hurt and anger; a somewhat detached, amused, intellectual analysis of the situation; and a third line of focus in which I looked "back" with some compassion from another viewpoint on a creature whose experience contained that kind of dilemma. This last level didn't feel either the emotions or the intellectual questions, but was aware of each and not caught up in the problem. The very next instant, the first verse of *Dialogues* sprang fully into my mind [*Dialogues of The Soul and Mortal Self in Time*, pp. ix–x].

She went on to write four poems within an hour and a half, and then stopped, thinking she was finished. But as the days went by, whole poems sprang to mind, and she wrote them down in what she described as an accelerated state of consciousness. She experienced her emotions directly, as if the dialogue were a real-life event, and through this felt a sense of catharsis, a resolution. The process lasted for about three months until she knew the dialogues were over. She looks back on the writing of the book as a peak experience. Here is one of the poems she wrote:

Dialogue Two: The Squirrel
Ah love
this mortal self who listens
and says, "Dear soul,
your marble words
go rolling through my bones,
from the mountains of my thoughts
down to my toes.
Your words are cold.
There is a language of the flesh
that I share with beast and bird,
a corporeal anxiety
built into creaturehood
that you don't know.

And yet
just now I watched a squirrel.
He perched on a tiny branch
that thrashed in the winter wind,
and ate some seed.
You didn't see him afraid
of falling off
or praying to his soul
for a better hold.
Perched atop his own mortality, he knew,
like some small furry god, secure
in a secret heaven of creaturehood
I've lost,
omnipotent in his own
processes.

Why should I envy him?
The squirrel can't write a poem.

He doesn't even know it's three o'clock.
Yesterday might as well not be
for all he can recall of it.
Yet he seems bristly
with a divinity I haven't got,
eternal and alive at once,
so ignorant
of his own mortality he'll live forever,
till his death, at least,
which won't impinge on him one bit, and so
has no reality.

How can he be so dumb
and live so well?"

The soul says, "Dear me,
I didn't realize
that you were in such a state.
Why don't you say that you're the lowliest creature
in the universe,
and be done with it?
The trouble is that you see
but you don't look.

As for the squirrel,
he knows no duration.
Even if he lives a thousand years,
his minutes disappear as if they never were.
His creature clarity is blessed
by instant cancellation
of his past
and where he is, is always.

And more:
The squirrel's unknowing is the same
that allows you to speak your name,
though the cells within your lips
are ignorant of the alphabet
you learned in school.
As far as unknowing is concerned,
you don't even know how your body moves
its solid stuff from room to room.

On top of that, you leap
the branches of the months and weeks,
keep your footing, waking or asleep,
while swinging high in the jungle treetops
of your chirruping memories.
But all of this you ignore
in your blind envy of the squirrel.
He has his world and you have yours.

Your thoughts emerge
from the landscape of your mind
as easily as trees spring up outside.
Your intellect rides high, a moving
moon in that inner sky,
to illuminate the unknowing wisdom of the eye
that sees without knowing how
and does not question why [Dialogues, pp. 7–11].

In this exercise you are going to write your own dialogue, between seeming opposite parts of your self, and see if you can resolve their differences. These might be the ego and the inner self, the parent and the child, the mind and the body, the rational self and the intuitive self, the masculine side and the feminine side—or perhaps two selves you have met in your dreams.

As we saw, Jane was inspired to start *Dialogues* through an incident in which she experienced strong emotions and also the sensation of being a detached observer of the emotional person. If you can recall an episode in your own life when you experienced strong emotion—whether or not you were also aware of a detached observer—this might be a starting point for your dialogue.

Write this in your journal, and try to let yourself experience your feelings as you do so, as if the situation portrayed were actually taking place. Don't try to force the dialogue; listen for what comes into your mind, and write it down. After you are finished, if you don't feel a sense of resolution just from the experience of writing the dialogue, list the beliefs that were expressed by both sides. See if you can find connections between them, much as you did in the previous exercise on opposites.

14

Value Fulfillment

Value fulfillment is a psychological and physical propensity that exists in each unit of consciousness, propelling it towards its own greatest fulfillment in such a way that its individual fulfillment also adds to the best possible development on the part of each other such unit of consciousness [*The Individual and The Nature of Mass Events*, p. 277].

Each of us—including the animals, plants, and atoms—is born with the feeling that we are something special. Feeling at the center of life, we can hardly conceive of a different, equally valid viewpoint from ours. No one else has quite the same perspective. We are born, too, with the secure sense that we fit perfectly into our environment, and with the desire to explore and expand and fulfill ourselves. This impetus toward "value fulfillment" as Seth calls it, is simply a desire to improve the *quality* of whatever form of life we find ourselves at the center of—to enrich that life in whatever way we can, through our own unique propensities, and in so doing leave our mark. As we have seen, we each have our own ideal psychological pattern, our own blueprint for growth that propels us toward the greatest possible value fulfillment for ourselves—and which, at the same time, leads to the enrichment of other life forms.

Survival, then—survival at any cost—is not enough for any of us. Life must have meaning. We can become deranged if we lose this feeling of being at life's center, of being safe and in control of our actions, of being a meaningful force in the scheme of things. The satisfaction of basic needs is not enough. We must also feel safe and free enough to be creative; to use our vitality to seek meaning in our lives through an intensification and fullfillment of whatever qualities we possess. We are not just an organism reacting to stimuli but have a built-in impulse toward growth and value fullfillment.

In this exercise, you will be taking a look at the values that are important to you, that give meaning to your life. In doing so, you should get insights into your particular "ideal psychological pattern" that resides in Framework 2 and which the inner self continually impels you toward developing.

How important is it that you possess (or work toward the development of) the following values? Rate each one on a scale of 1 to 5, with 1 being "not important" and 5 being "extremely important." (Add to the list any other values that are important to you.)

1. a good education
2. ample opportunity for travel
3. artistic achievement
4. contentment
5. a satisfying sexual relationship
6. good health
7. close family ties
8. strength
9. a beautiful body
10. wealth
11. fame
12. athletic ability
13. a worthy cause
14. companionship
15. spiritual growth
16. a sense of humor
17. curiosity
18. manual dexterity
19. sensitivity
20. discipline
21. solitude
22. passion
23. good eyesight
24. good hearing
25. popularity
26. a devoted mate
27. attractiveness
28. personal freedom
29. loyalty to country
30. masculinity/femininity
31. romantic love
32. religious faith
33. self-esteem
34. a pleasing personality
35. honesty
36. admiration
37. genius
38. courage

39. composure
40. patience
41. gentleness
42. a way with words

The next step is to list in your journal all the values you rated 5 and then to rank these in order of importance, with the most important value at the top and the least important at the bottom. Since you have rated *all* of these values as "very important," this may be difficult to do, but through forcing yourself to make a choice from among your most important values, you will find out a great deal about what really matters to you.

After you have done that, examine in your journal the development of the values that are most important to you (and any others you want to look at). What beliefs do you have in regard to each value? What emotions do you feel when you think of that particular value? What beliefs are behind the emotions? Are any of these beliefs limiting? When in the past did you first become aware of (the development of) that value? What steps have you taken to develop it? What are you doing now? What do you envision in the future?

End by writing a poem entitled: "A Life of Meaning." Use whatever images come to mind.

15

Memory Refresher
#1

The past contains for each of you some moments of joy, strength, creativity and splendor, as well as episodes of unhappiness, despair perhaps, turmoil and cruelty. Your present convictions will act like a magnet, activating all such past issues, happy or sad. You will choose from your previous experience all of those events that reinforce your conscious beliefs, and so ignore those that do not; the latter may even seem to be nonexistent ... the emerging memories will then turn on the body mechanisms, merging past and present in some kind of harmonious picture. This means that the pieces will fit together whether they are joyful or not.

This joining of the past and present, in that context, predisposes you to similar future events, for you have geared yourself for them. Change now quite practically alters both the past and the future [*The Nature of Personal Reality*, pp. 339–40].

Have you ever noticed that when you are thinking about a past event, you take on, to some extent, the feelings that you had at the time? You think about an embarrassing episode and feel embarrassed all over again. Recounting a moment of triumph makes you feel triumphant once more. This is what Seth means when he talks about memories turning on the body mechanisms, and "merging past and present in some kind of harmonious picture." By thinking about the past, in other words, you actually change your present and gear yourself up for similar events in the future.

The implications of this are obvious: if you want to create a more pleasant present and future for yourself, don't dwell on unpleasant thoughts of the past. Focus instead on positive, pleasant times, and use them to reinforce the present.

This is the first of two exercises whose purpose is to get you in touch with past experiences that were pleasurable, affirming ones for you. As Seth says, we tend to choose experiences from the past that reinforce our present beliefs and ignore others. Thus, if we are feeling down on ourselves we will tend to look back and recall other past times when we felt the same way— which only reinforces the present feeling. By doing these exercises, you will build up a repertoire of pleasurable incidents from which to draw. When you are feeling down about something, rather than recalling unpleasant incidents, you can refer to these, concentrate on one, and actually bring into your present some of those good feelings from the past.

Don't try to do all the items in this exercise in one time period. Set aside fifteen to twenty minutes each day for it, until you have used all the items that bring to mind pleasurable incidents. For each item, close your eyes and picture the scene happening as you remember it. *Feel* yourself there. Smell the smells, taste the tastes. Savor each delicious moment. Then let the scene fade and feel the effects of those pleasurable emotions on your body now. Feel the energy surge through you. Imagine yourself feeling just as good in the future.

Remember a time when:

- you were praised for a job well done
- you laughed and laughed and laughed
- you fell in love
- you were very moved by someone
- a dream came true
- you enjoyed a beautiful sunset
- everything fell into place
- you were totally satisfied
- you won
- you really appreciated someone
- you indulged yourself
- you felt relieved
- you felt at one with the universe
- you felt cherished
- you savored a warm bed and clean sheets
- you played hookey
- you had an "aha!" experience
- you were first choice
- you had a massage
- you didn't care what other people thought
- you were fascinated by something
- you made peace with someone
- you overcame your fear
- you enjoyed doing absolutely nothing
- you were happy
- you acted courageously
- someone comforted you
- you felt playful as a child
- you realized how much you knew

16

Belief Assignment #3

You are overweight. You have tried diets to no avail. You tell yourself that you want to lose weight. You follow what I have said so far. You change the belief. You say, "Because I believe I am overweight, I am, so I will think of myself at my ideal weight."

But you find that you still overeat. In your mind's eye you see yourself as overweight, imagine the goodies and snacks, and in your terms "give in" to your imagination—and you think that will power is useless and conscious thought powerless.

But pretend that you go beyond this point ... you say, "All right, I will examine my beliefs further!" You may ... find that you believe you are not worthy ... or that health means physical weight ... that you are so vulnerable that you need the weight so people will think twice before they shove you around. In all cases, the ideas will be conscious. You have entertained them often and your imagination and emotions are in league with them, and *not* in conflict [*The Nature of Personal Reality*, pp. 86–7].

For this third belief assignment, write down in your journal beliefs about yourself in the following areas: *how I appear to the world, how the world reacts to me, how I appear to myself, how I react to myself.*

Again start with the "facts"—your age, sex, height, weight, your marital status, your education, your job background. Then think about these "facts." What influence does the "fact" that you are a certain age have on other people? On yourself? Do you or others think of you as old or young, past your prime, too youthful to be taken seriously? Ask yourself questions like this about each of the facts. Then go on to describe your personality, your character, your skills, abilities, accomplishments, likes and dislikes, your relationships with others, and so on. Try not to emphasize what you consider to be your limiting or negative beliefs about yourself here, though. Also include positive, unlimiting beliefs.

For this exercise, try to perceive what role your imagination plays in your beliefs about yourself. What pictures do you have in your mind? Do these pictures match the beliefs you have listed? If not, re-examine your beliefs. You may find others behind them that are in keeping with your imagination. Realize that by changing the picture in your mind, you can also change your beliefs.

17

On Affirming
the Emotions

...You must accept the emotional self, not superficially, not idealistically, but as it now exists: the reality of what you are *now* — and then you can begin to work with what you are and what you have. The self is immediate as All That Is is immediate, and your quickest entry point is at the point of your present feelings, and there is no other way. The door to your feelings is open by accepting your feelings, at this moment, or at any moment ... [*Conversations with Seth*, Vol. 1, p. 86].

As we have seen, emotions are a type of impulse and as such, are a direct connection with Framework 2, which contains our ideal psychological pattern. It is in Framework 2 that the inner self operates, processing the information it constantly receives in the form of aware-ized energy, selecting and translating the information that is relevant and beneficial to us, and sending it to Framework 1 for the ego to act upon.

But all too often we don't act upon the impulses we receive, especially if the impulse is in the form of an emotion. We have come to fear our emotions, afraid that if we let them out, "the floodgates will burst open" and we will be annihilated—or annihilate someone else. But fearing our emotions may ultimately lead to more drastic consequences than expressing them would, since anxiety added to the original emotion only intensifies it.

The reason there is so much power behind blocked impulses of any kind is that feelings pile up on one another. Say, for instance, that you feel yourself becoming angry about something, but because you think it is bad to be angry, you repress it. You still feel the unexpressed anger within you (though perhaps not consciously—it may now be in the form of a headache or back pain or depression), which makes you feel powerless. That feeling gives an extra charge to the original feeling of anger. On top of that, you fear you may still let out that bad emotion, so *that* feeling, too, adds its charge to the original anger. Thus an emotion builds that would, if expressed immediately, quickly dissipate. As the pressure mounts within you, you find yourself thinking murderous thoughts, which makes you feel both guilty and afraid. You repress the murderous thoughts, the guilt and the fear, adding yet more pressure to the original denied impulse ... and so on, to the point where you develop an ulcer, have a migraine headache, sink into severe depression, or commit armed robbery.

It isn't likely that just *one* incident of repression would lead to such dire consequences, but the point is, we are constantly repressing emotions, and must find something to relieve the accumulated pressure. Ironically, one of our main reasons for repressing emotions is that we have seen situations where anger or hatred erupted in violence. This seems to be proof that emotions are dangerous and not to be trusted. But in actuality, what is dangerous is *not* the expression of the emotion as it arises naturally out of the impulses, but its repression. The spontaneous expression of emotion is never a violent act.

Seth makes a distinction between aggression and violence. Aggression is creative in nature; it is energy directed toward a goal, and often serves as a communication to *prevent* violence. He uses the example of animals who bare their teeth or growl in order to express their hostile feelings toward other animals. This is a ritualized act of communication, serving to prevent violence rather than to initiate it. Violence is quite the opposite. It is an act of surrender to the overwhelming power of repressed emotions, and is destructive. While in an aggressive situation, then, we have control over our energy and power, in a violent situation we don't. The energy runs wild and dissipates.

We need to understand more fully this connection between creativity and aggression. We tend to think of creativity as something that "just comes"—as something that happens *to* us rather than as something we bring about. But creativity is what we *do* with what "just comes"—what we do with our impulses. Creativity is the result of aggression, of directing our energy toward a goal—a goal that has "just come" to us through our impulses, be that goal to laugh uproariously, to turn our back on someone, to write a sonnet, or in some other way to *communicate* our impulse—to make it manifest in physical reality. An act of creativity, then, is an act of communication of our impulses, and aggression is simply the perpetrator of this act. It is the use of power to create. Violence, on the other hand, is the use of power to destroy.

Unfortunately we tend to associate power with violence and destruction. We don't realize that we are constantly using our energy/power creatively and that the few occasions when power goes astray are the exception, not the rule. Of course it's frightening when this happens because we feel so helpless, so out of control. It seems that power has the upper hand and there is nothing we can do about it. But the solution is not to hide from the power, to ignore and repress it, but to keep it flowing. It is harmful only when it builds up, not when it is being put to use as it becomes available.

Another effect of repressing our emotions is that we lose touch with our conscious beliefs. Our emotions rise out of our beliefs, and when expressed show us what we think about something; when they are repressed, we are deprived of valuable feedback. We cannot hope to take conscious charge in this business of reality-creating if we are unaware of what our beliefs are. And we cannot be aware of our beliefs if we repress the emotions which symbolize them.

Emotions, then, like other impulses are messages; meant to tell us something. Until we express them, we cannot know what that message is. We need to trust the fact that there *is* a message in the emotions—that they are not just arbitrary, meaningless feelings, but a symbolization of beliefs that we have. Any emotion, *felt and faced*, will automatically reveal its message. You will understand why you felt the way you did. You will see the belief behind the emotion, which will explain your reaction. And once you understand this, the emotion will change into something else. For e-motions are always in motion.

This does not mean, though, that if you are angry at people, you should necessarily yell at them or in other ways express your anger in their presence. This is not always a wise thing to do. But you *can* recognize that you are angry and, if possible, isolate yourself and pound on a pillow or express it physically in some other way. The angry feelings will soon subside and the message will reveal itself to you. It will undoubtedly have to do with something you fear. For what motivates all—repeat, *all*—so-called negative behavior is fear. And the fear is a result of not trusting yourself.

For instance, say you are angry at a friend for not having followed through on a promise. You helped him with a task and he promised to help you in exchange, but didn't appear on the day it had to be done. This really makes you mad. You vividly fantasize beating him to a pulp and enjoy every minute of it. You can *feel* yourself doing it and relish it. After a while the fantasy fades and you feel calm, relaxed and in harmony, for in going along with your feelings you have *unified* mind and body. And in this state, you realize that you were angry because you had feared your ability to do the task by yourself; it is something you have avoided because you didn't feel capable of doing it by yourself. You realize that your friend's failure to follow through on his promise is a blessing in disguise, for now you have the opportunity to learn to do something new and thus add to your feeling of competence and self-worth. Every time you let your "negative" emotions run their course, you will find that there is a perfectly understandable belief behind them—a belief you otherwise might not have been aware of.

Hate is an emotion that many people fear or feel guilty about because all too often it is directed at an intimate other. This *is* scary; it seems "bad" to feel this way. It must mean we don't really love that person. What a phony we are! But oh, how we resent that person for making us feel this way! And so the sentences go on in our head. As Seth says, though, hatred is akin to love, for both are based on self-identification. In the case of both love and hate, we *identify* with the object of our love or hate, be it a person or ideal. When we hate, it is because we feel painfully separated from the love. (That is, our *fear* —our belief—is that we are painfully separated from it.) Seth uses the example of children who say to a parent: "I hate you." The message behind the message is "I love you so. Why are you so mean to me?" [*The Nature of Personal Reality*, p. 475]. If parents can understand this, they won't try to suppress or punish a child for such a statement, for, expressed, hatred will turn back into love. But left to fester, it could erupt into violence.

The emotions are one of the most concentrated forms of energy we possess—a powerful source of creativity and learning. Following them leads to valuable insights about ourselves. We must trust our emotions and trust ourselves. We must say "yes" to ourselves and to our life and accept our own uniqueness. We must *affirm* ourselves. As Seth says

> Affirmation of yourself is one of your greatest strengths. You can at times quite properly deny certain portions of experience while still confirming your own vitality. You do not have to say "yes" to people, issues, or events with which you are deeply disturbed. Affirmation does not mean a bland wishy-washy acceptance of anything that comes your way, regardless of your feelings about it ... emotions ... are natural, ever-changing states of feeling, each leading into another ... to refuse them is futile ... emotions simply *are* ... you cannot affirm one emotion and deny another without setting up barriers. You try to hide what you think of as negative feelings in the closet of your mind, as in the past they closeted insane relatives. All of this because you do not trust the aspects of your individuality in flesh. Affirmation means accepting your soul as it appears in creaturehood ... you cannot deny your creaturehood without denying your soul .... Affirmation then, is the acquiescence to your ability as a spirit within flesh to form the physical reality of your creaturehood. [*The Nature of Personal Reality*, pp. 466, 467, 468, 495].

This exercise is an uncomplicated one: simply affirm yourself. Do it often. Affirm your emotions, affirm the events in your life, look in the mirror and affirm your*self*. Any time you find yourself feeling anxious or confused, say to yourself, "This is *my* life, and I form it." Realize that your emotions are tools to use in forming that life, that they are a useful and valuable means by which to know yourself better. Welcome them and affirm them and affirm *yourself*.

18

An Inventory
of Successes

Now I don't mean to stress the negative by any means, so I suggest that you look to those areas of your life in which you are pleased and have done well. See how emotionally and imaginatively you personally reinforced those beliefs, and brought them to physical fruition—realize how naturally and automatically the results appeared. Catch hold of those feelings of accomplishment and understand that you can use the same methods in other areas [*The Nature of Personal Reality*, p. 88].

We are so busy looking at the defects and lacks in our lives that we fail to notice our strengths and accomplishments. We take for granted, for instance, the "fact" that we have a strong and healthy body, while bewailing the "fact" that we don't get paid enough for the work we do. Occasionally we will be reminded of what we have by someone who doesn't have it, and for a moment see ourselves from a different perspective. But soon we return to our accustomed focus on failings.

Yet as Seth repeatedly points out, this focus on negatives only serves to reinforce our belief that we are incomplete, and thus perpetuates that reality. This applies to both thoughts of the past and thoughts of the present. For when we constantly view ourselves as having been and still being defective in various ways, we set up expectations for the future. We get what we concentrate on.

Not that we should gloss over those aspects of ourselves we are dissatisfied with, though, for we need to explore our beliefs and feelings in those areas so we'll know what changes we want to make. A careful examination of the contents of our mind is absolutely necessary if we hope to be conscious reality-creators. But to dwell on what we believe to be our past and present failings is to perpetuate them. We need to remember our strengths and to remind ourselves of all the successes we have.

In this exercise, you are going to take inventory of the many successes you have had in your life, and take a look at how you achieved what you did. You will then be able to use these techniques more consciously in the future.

In your journal, make a list of everything about your life you feel positive or at least neutral—rather than negative—about. Skills, accomplishments, interpersonal relationships, personality, appearance, health, environment, money, and possessions. Be as detailed and comprehensive as you can. Don't forget things like being able to type or drive a car, for our major achievements are always the result of a series of small steps accomplished over a period of time. Every aspect of your reality is there because you created it, so take a look at it with that in mind. Do you have friendly neighbors? Then pat yourself on the back for having created that reality for yourself. Do children take to you? Put that down. Do you have a great view from your window? Add that to your list. Also think about things you have *improved* in over time, even if you tend not yet to be fully satisfied with yourself in that area, *e.g.*, "I am much less shy than I used to be," or "I burn the dinner only once a week now."

You will, I think, be surprised, as I was when I did this exercise, at what a long list you can come up with, a list of mostly "invisible" taken-for-granted things that you have done successfully in creating this reality for yourself. Think for a moment—but don't dwell on—what your life would be like if you hadn't created these many things. Then think of what it *is* like now because of them. Feel a sense of appreciation for what you've done.

Now go back over your list and choose those items you are particularly pleased about, or which seem most basic, most important to the quality of your life. For each item, write down all the beliefs you can think of that went into the creation of that reality for yourself. Then think of how your imagination reinforced this belief. Think back on the pictures in your mind, on the fantasies that led you to the creation of that reality. Think, too, of the emotions that went along with and supported your beliefs in this area. Can you see how your beliefs, imagination, and emotions all worked together to create that reality?

After you have examined all of the items in this manner, see if you can come up with some guidelines for yourself, to be used for future creations. Can you see patterns in all the situations that you can apply to future situations? Or perhaps you feel you were "just lucky" in achieving what you did. In that case, recognize and affirm your strong belief in luck.

Refer to this list regularly to remind yourself of what you have accomplished. Love and appreciate yourself for these successes.

19

A Visual Autobiography

You experience yourself in a certain way topside, so to speak, and so in order to take advantage of information at other levels of awareness, you must learn to experience those other organizational systems with which you are usually unfamiliar.... First of all, these other organizations do not deal primarily with time at all, but with the emotions and associative processes.... Thoughts of your own next birthday, for instance, may instantly lead you to think of past ones, or a series of birthday pictures may come to mind of your own twelfth birthday, your third, your seventh, in an order uniquely your own. That order will be determined by emotional associations.... You remember only significant events or details. Your emotions trigger your memories, and they organize your associations. Your emotions are generated through your beliefs. They attach themselves so that certain beliefs and emotions seem almost synonymous ... [*The Nature of The Psyche*, pp. 47–9].

The information that comes to us directly from Framework 2—through dreams, impulses, hunches and the like—is organized differently from the information we receive through the physical senses in our Framework 1 reality. We perceive physical events as happening in time, one following the other and thus, when we recount our experiences, we automatically organize them in time sequences. We are so tied to the concept of time that it is difficult to grasp other types of organization. That is why our dreams may seem so puzzling, or why we cannot understand the reason for an impulse. For the information coming to us from Framework 2 is organized through association. Events will not be ordered according to time but by their emotional associations.

Thus, as we saw in Seth's example, your future birthday may remind you of your twelfth birthday, then your third, then your seventh and so on in an order that makes no sense to the "logical" time-oriented mind, but which makes perfect sense to the inner self, who is trying to tell "us" (our ego) something—and as usual, something that it would be beneficial for us to understand and act on.

For this reason, then—the fact that the inner self is trying to tell us something that would further our development—we need to learn to translate these messages, since the more tools we have to understanding the way our mind works, the better. Actually, we are already familiar with our associative processes, not only through our dreams but through our waking reveries, at times when our "monitor for logic" isn't operating and we just let the associations flow. We do this all the time, and the process adds valuable input to our decisions and actions, just as our dreams do, but not usually on a conscious level. To become more conscious reality-creators, we must give more attention to the familiar associative process and learn to interpret emotional connections that are made. This exercise will give you practice in doing that.

In your journal, list all the important events in your life, in chronological order. These events must be important to *you*, even if they would have little significance to someone else. If all your birthdays were meaningful, indicate them. If some weren't, include only those that were. Now, if you have note cards, use those; if not, make some cards by cutting blank sheets of typing paper into as many 3 by 5 inch pieces as you have events. On each piece, write a word or draw a symbol that will bring to mind that one particular event—a heart, a birthday cake, a key word, and so forth. If you have old photographs depicting some of these events, use these instead of the cards or pieces of paper.

Now arrange the cards on a flat surface, from left to right, comic-book style, in chronological order. You now have a visual autobiography of your life, in the usual order that autobiographies follow. Now reverse the order of the cards so that the event that came first in the upper left-hand corner is last in the lower right-hand corner. You now have a backwards view of your life. This may give you some insights you hadn't had before. If so, make note of them in your journal.

Now choose the event that arouses the strongest emotions in you. This event may not have been especially emotional at the time, but in any case, choose the one you *now* feel most emotional about. Take this card and, pushing the other cards aside to form a rough circle, place it in the center. Look at it closely and vividly imagine the scene as it took place in the past. Imagine it growing in size and intensity.

Now let this scene attract to it others from around the circle. Let these scenes connect with the central scene and attract others. Feel their connection, their emotional connections with one another. Keep doing this—arranging and rearranging the picture until you sense a unity among all the parts.

Now write in your journal about the experience, as if you were interpreting a dream. Pay special attention to the emotional content of all the events and their interconnections with one another. Try to perceive the beliefs behind the emotions, the beliefs that generated the emotions. What do they have in common? See if you can bring to conscious awareness (if you haven't already) the message behind the arrangement you made. But don't try to force it into words if words don't come. Words aren't essential **to** understanding.

Do this exercise every now and again, each time making up a new chronological list, because the events that stand out in your mind will change from one time to another.

20

Sending Love
to "Earlier" Selves

Seth says that even in this life, each of us has various egos; we only accept the idea of one ego as a sort of shorthand symbolism. The ego at any given time in this life is simply the part of us that "surfaces;" a group of characteristics that the inner self uses to solve various problems. Even the ego as we think of it changes constantly. For example, the Jane Roberts of now is different from the Jane Roberts of ten years ago, though "I" have not been conscious of any particular change of identity [*The Seth Material,* p. 234].

In a sense, your lifetime is a series of reincarnational existences. The self you are now is not the self you were when you were six or twelve or twenty, or the self you were even a year ago. You look back with a sense of nostalgia and empathy on the you of before and think "If I only knew then what I know now." You realize you are a different person from what you were because of the learning experiences you have been through—because of the learning experiences those earlier selves went through. These selves are a part of you, you recognize—the child is still there, within, and the adolescent, and the struggling young adult—yet they are not "you." You "contain" them and yet you are not simply the sum of those parts. You are uniquely *you.*

Central to the theory of reincarnation is the concept of karma—the idea that your present self is responsible for the acts of past selves and must atone for their wrongdoing—and this concept, too can be applied to a single lifetime. You realize that you have developed behavior patterns over the years, some of which continue to serve you well, and others that have only led to pain and alienation. You realize that here and now, one of your tasks is to grow out of those restricting patterns that you set up earlier. So in that sense, you have inherited a karmic debt from your earlier selves and must pay if off. You can see what it is that you have set up for yourself to learn, just in this lifetime, not to mention previous lifetimes.

But of course, what Seth says about reincarnation and karma applies in this situation as well. Since time does not exist, all reincarnational lives, and all the selves of this lifetime, exist simultaneously, right now. This means that a "future" life can influence a "past" life as well as the other way around, so karma in its usual sense does not apply. The point is, though, that our various selves *do* influence one another. Since they all exist "now," there is constant interaction among them. If one self, whether "future" or "past," does something harmful, all the other selves will be affected by it. And if one does something beneficial, the same rule applies.

You saw in the memory refresher exercise how a pleasant memory will actually cause changes in your body right now, bringing into the "present" the surge of exuberant energy experienced at that point in the "past." This is direct evidence that one self can influence another. It is happening all the time whether or not you are conscious of it. And it works both ways. If you can be renewed and replenished through tuning in to the positive energy of a past self, you can also renew and replenish that past self by sending it positive energy from the present. In doing so, you will automatically be renewing and replenishing yourself, since in a sense you *are* that self of the past.

In this exercise, you will send strength and love to those "earlier" selves of yours who seem to need it right "now." For this you can use the series of events you used in the last exercise as a starting point. Or you can make up a new list of significant events in your life. In any case, go over these incidents, and as you do, clearly visualize the self you were then who was experiencing each incident. How did you feel at that point in time? Was it a time of exuberance and joy in your life, or was it a time of fear and indecision in which you could have used some love and encouragement?

Now, for those selves you meet who need help, go through the following process. Imagine them standing before you. Look deeply into the eyes of each of these selves and communicate love and encouragement. Put your arms around them and hold them close. Rock them in your arms and tell them how dear they are to you, how much you have learned from them. Let them know how important they are to you, and how much they have accomplished. Tell them that their troubles will soon be over and that everything will work out—that you are *proof* that everything has worked out. Tell them that you are sending them energy and that they will feel it surging through them. Tell them that any time they need you, all they need do is ask and you will be there for them. Give each of them a big hug and say good-bye.

Just as with the memory refresher exercise, you will find from doing this exercise that you feel energized and refreshed. For by giving to the other selves, you are giving to yourself.

21

Belief Assignment
#4

Physical existence is valuable for many reasons, one being that the flesh is so responsive to thought and yet so resilient. There are built-in guidelines so that the body consciousness itself, while mirroring your negative images at times, will also automatically struggle against them.

You must remember that you dwell always in a natural framework—which means that your thoughts themselves are as natural, say, as the locks of your hair. In what may seem to you to be an odd analogy, I will compare your thoughts with viruses, for they are alive, always present, responsive, and possess their own kind of mobility. Physically speaking, at least, thoughts are chemically propelled, and they travel through the universal body as viruses travel through your temporal form. Thoughts interact with the body and become part of it as viruses do [*The Nature of Personal Reality*, pp. 140–1].

For this fourth belief assignment, write down in your journal all of your thoughts about "The Body." Not your *own* body, but bodies in general. What are some ideas you have picked up over the years about The Body? Think of sculptures and paintings you have seen of bodies. What has been your reaction to them? What are your feelings about bodies in general? What are your beliefs behind these feelings?

Now, what are your beliefs about health? In general, again. What is your opinion of unhealthy people? What is behind these opinions? How do foods affect health? What do you think about medicine and doctors?

Now write down your gut feelings about your own body. How do you feel about your body—its appearance, how well it functions, its strengths and weaknesses? What are your feelings about your own health? What beliefs are behind these feelings?

Compare your beliefs about *the* body and *your* body. Are there differences? Do you feel in general that the body is miraculous, but that nature somehow botched it up when producing yours? If so, you have an example there of the difference between intellectual assumptions and emotional assumptions. Intellectual assumptions are based on what you think you should believe—the official viewpoint. Emotional assumptions are indicators of your true beliefs—often quite different.

Now compare your beliefs about health in general and your health. Do you believe in "naturally good health" for everyone but yourself? Do you find yourself critical of unhealthy people but very sympathetic with yourself when you are ill? Or is it the other way around? What do these discrepancies say about your true beliefs vis à vis health? What can you do to change the beliefs that affect you adversely?

22

An Exercise in Imagination

The psyche ... not only has no one sexual identification, but it is the larger psychic and psychological bank of potential from which all gradations of sexuality emerge. It is not asexual, and yet it is the combination of those richest ingredients considered to be male and female.

The human personality is therefore endowed sexually and psychologically with a freedom from *strict* sexual orientation. This has contributed to the survival of the species by not separating any of its mental or psychological abilities into two opposite camps. Except for the physical processes of reproduction, the species is free to arrange its psychological characteristics in whatever fashions it chooses [*The Nature of The Psyche*, p. 186].

How programmed are we in our sexual beliefs and orientation? A good way to get some insights into this question is to do an exercise Seth suggests in *The Nature of the Psyche*.

Think of a recent incident in which you were aware of sexual conventions. You saw different roles being played by male and female. Recall your behavior and the behavior of the member of the opposite sex. Now, playfully imagine yourself in a similar situation in which the sexes are reversed and you are of the opposite sex. Really get into the role and *be* that person. What are you thinking? What are you feeling? Write the scenario in your journal.

Afterwards, examine your feeling about playing that role. What do those feelings reveal about your beliefs? If you are a parent, how would your attitude and behavior toward your children change if you were of the opposite sex?

23

Multipersonhood
and Latent Abilities

... "you" are aware of only one small portion of yourself, and this portion you protect as your identity ... The body that you have is a probable body. It is the result of one line of "development" that could be taken by your particular earth personality in the flesh. All the other possible lines of development also occur, however ... each one simultaneously affects every other.... Because you are a probable self ... you can draw from your own bank of probable abilities ... being developed in another reality.... In terms of time, *you* have many bodies, as you are born and reborn in earth experience. Your consciousness straddles those existences, and even the atoms and the molecules within your present body contain the coded knowledge of those other (really simultaneous) forms.... Both biologically and psychically, then, you are aware of your multipersonhood [*The "Unknown" Reality,* Vol. 1, pp. 68, 69, 71, 79].

The whole self is a gestalt of energy. At any "point in time," some of that energy is manifest in physical form and some is unmanifest. The unmanifest portion is what we call the inner self or the inner ego, the spiritual self or the soul.

This entity, desiring to know itself through its creations, is continually directing its energy into physical manifestation. Each pulse of its energy, each hum of desire, gives birth to myriad beings and scatters them along a time continuum in physical reality. These beings are called reincarnational selves. Each is a unique version of the inner self in the flesh, each with its own personality and its own abilities for growth, yet united to all others through a single creator, and single thought—a single pulse of desire.

As it grows and develops, each of these selves is continually making choices among various courses of action—probable actions. Whenever a self chooses to follow a certain path, other versions of that self verge off from it to follow the paths *not* taken in a different system of reality—a probable system. Logically enough, Seth calls these entities probable selves. Probable selves are just as "real" as the reincarnational selves, possessed of their own unique viewpoint and propensities, and united with the others through the inner self.

This is what is meant by "multipersonhood." While each of us maintains our own identity in time and space, each of us is at the same time part of a larger whole, consisting not only of the inner self but of innumerable other selves the inner self manifests. In a sense, then, we all share the same mind. Seth compared the situation to a case of split personality in which one body is occupied by several distinct personalities, each one unaware of all the others, each one thinking that it is the only true personality, the only true physical representation of inner reality.

However, we are only a small portion of the whole self—the portion we identify as "I," one personality in a vast gestalt of personalities, all rising from the same source, all familiar with the same inner self.

Rather than give you an inferiority complex, though, this concept should encourage you, for it means that we all have access to the ideas, abilities, and experiences of all our "fellow" personalities through our common connection to the inner self. We should be able to pick up on and learn from those other entities.

And of course, this is happening all the time on an unconscious level. The inner self is continually feeding us information—much of it about the learning and achievements of the other selves—that we can use for our growth. Any time we feel a vague yearning toward a certain skill or achievement, it means that one or more of our other selves is developing that skill in another reality. The inner self does the best it can to help us take advantage of all these "latent abilities," but we are of course free to choose *not* to. When we believe in the limited I-self, we can't take full advantage of these opportunities, for all we see is our limitations. If we are to become more conscious reality-creators, we need to recognize that there are *no* limitations to the self; that we have an infinite store of knowledge and experience to draw from. All we have to do is ask the inner self to make it available to us. But first we have to *believe* this is indeed the case. Once we believe it, then it's only a matter of deciding in ourselves which abilities we want to develop.

The purpose of this exercise is to get you in touch with your latent abilities and to get you started on actualizing some of them. Do you find yourself resisting the idea that there are no limits to what you can do? For the purpose of this exercise, try to suspend your belief in limits and playfully pretend that you *can* do anything you want. Once you see that you *can* achieve your goals this way, your belief in limits will automatically fall away.

Part One

In your journal, make a list of all the hobbies you had as a child, all the secondary abilities you now have—things you have enjoyed doing or are pretty good at, but never did much with; all the things you have said maybe you'll do some day if only you have the time. What achievements do you feel drawn toward in others? What personality traits do you particularly enjoy in others (for example, common sense or good memory)? What do you daydream about? List all these things.

Each item you have listed represents a latent ability that you could develop. Go through them and see if there are common elements among the items. Can you find a series of sub-skills that, together, could add up to one generalized skill? Are there any other patterns or groupings in evidence?

Part Two

Now choose one *small* item to work on, something you could develop fairly well in a short time. If one of your cravings is to write the Great American Novel, put that on the back burner for now, and choose something less ambitious. For example, would you perhaps like to develop a better sense of humor?

Then plan to do something each day toward developing this skill. In the case of a sense of humor, this might be to pause and reflect at a given time each day on the humor of the situation you happen to be in at that moment. Try to keep what you do as uncomplicated as possible, something that takes no more than five minutes a day to accomplish. Tell yourself that you will do this thing *each* day, playfully, and that you won't look for results until at least two weeks have gone by. Do not think in terms of results. Just realize, know, that you are developing one of your latent abilities, and that over a period of time that ability will become manifest.

At the end of two weeks, assess your progress. Decide if you want to continue on with your present plan, to change it, or to work on another ability in the same way.

24

Predicting
the Future

Continue to rely upon known channels of information, but implement these and begin to explore the unrecognized ones also available. What information do you have, for example, presently unknown to yourself? Try your hand at predicting future events. In the beginning, it does not matter whether or not your predictions are "true." You will be stretching your consciousness into areas usually unused. Do not put any great stake in your predictions, for if you do, you will be very disappointed if they do not work out.... If you continue, you will indeed discover that you are aware of some future events, when such knowledge is not available in usual terms.... There will be associative patterns that you follow successfully, leading toward "correct" precognitions. You will also discover that the emotions are highly involved in such procedures: You will perceive information that is significant to you for some reason. That significance will act like a magnet, attracting those data to you.

Now, in the normal course of events you attract experience in the same fashion. You anticipate events. You are aware of them before they happen, whether or not you ever succeed in conscious predictions [*The Nature of The Psyche*, pp. 52–3].

In our space-time reality we perceive experience in bits, one after the other. Seth likens us to travellers through a forest, encountering trees along the way. The ones we have gone by are "past," the ones we see around us are "present," and the ones up ahead which we can't yet see are "future." Yet all the trees exist at once—as would be obvious to a person in an airplane flying over the forest.

Past, present, and future exist simultaneously. Were this not the case, then how would it be possible to predict future events? But future events *have* been predicted, time and again. Scientists, lacking a theory to explain such phenomena, ascribe them to coincidence, but too many "coincidences" have occurred for this to be a plausible explanation. It really *is* possible to tune in to future events.

But the future is not foreordained. It is continually changing as the present—and past—changes. Whatever choice we make from our present point of power "will" alter future choices.

For instance, say you have the option of going to a party or staying home. At this point in time, your future consists of two sets of events—among others—one having to do with staying home and the other having to do with going to the party. Let's say you stay home. At this point the future changes—the set of events having to do with the party are no longer readily available to you. They are like a clump of trees off another path in the forest, which you can no longer see.

Even if you changed your mind at some point and decided to go to the party after all, the events would not be the same as those which existed previously. You'd have to leave your forest path and cut through the woods to the other path, seeing trees along the way you would not have seen otherwise. So the future is ever-changing. You can know the probabilities, but you can't know for sure which events will take place. Not even highly-gifted psychics can expect one hundred per cent accuracy in predicting future events. Still, we are constantly anticipating events—as Seth says, "attracting experiences"—through our expectations, whether we realize it or not. If we can become aware of how we do this, then to some extent we can have conscious control over the choices we make, or at the very least, come to understand what we perceive as "significant" to us—which events we can foresee.

In *How to Develop your ESP Power*, Jane Roberts tells of her own experiments with predicting the future. Over a period of six months, she made 741 predictions, of which 320 showed significant results—significant in that there didn't seem to be any reasonable explanation other than precognition for the predictions coming true. For the most part the events she predicted were quite ordinary, and yet not a usual part of the daily routine. For example, one day her predictions included: "a secret told," "a sharp tongue," and "a tease." That same day she was visited by the housekeeper of an elderly neighbor who told Jane she was going to quit working because that woman had "a very sharp tongue," and was continually "teasing" her. The housekeeper than proceeded to tell Jane a *secret* about the neighbor.

Later, when Jane started holding ESP classes, the class did the same experiment in predictions. As Sue Watkins recounts:

> On Monday, July 7, 1969, I wrote the following in my notebook for the next day—July 8:
>
> 1. Cataracts
> 2. An old friend will call you—you haven't seen him in a long time.
> 3. Salamanders
>
> On the next day, according to my notes, the following events occurred in this order:
>
> 1. I received the weekly Martha's Vineyard *Gazette* in the mail and read in it that a woman who used to help me write the social news for our village had been operated on for cataracts.

2. Darren Stephens, whom I had not heard from for more than a year, called at 6 P.M. from California.

3. Later in the evening, I drove to a local shopping mall and saw snakes and chameleons in the pet shop there. I like reptiles, but like many people, I confuse the orders within these classes. Salamanders are amphibians, chameleons are reptiles [*Conversations with Seth*, Vol. 1, pp. 75–76].

As these examples illustrate, we can predict future events, and without much effort. All it amounts to is jotting down whatever phrases come to mind, and then checking to see whether these jottings correlate with what happens later. Jane said that sometimes it would take three days before her predictions came true; other times, when they didn't happen, she would sometimes find out that they had *almost* happened—for instance, when she had predicted a visit for that day, a person was thinking of visiting her but changed his mind, and later told her so. Sometimes, then, the misses turn out to be hits after all—or at least near-misses.

Plan to do this exercise daily over a period of months. If you just do it once, or intermittently, you won't learn much from it. But if you do it regularly, you should be able to perceive patterns in your perceptions. You will be quite good at making some associations of events, not so good at others. Also, you will come to see that the events you predicted accurately had some sort of emotional significance to you.

Each day, then, make three to five quick predictions. Don't try to second-guess here, just write down whatever comes to mind, whether or not it makes sense. Include the date. Later—playfully, without any great stake in the results—check back and see if any of the predictions came to pass. Look on it as just a fun thing to do that doesn't take more than five minutes a day.

When you find you have a hit, be sure to make a note of it. Over a period of time, as you come to trust your impulses to write down "meaningless" words, your percentage of hits may go up. See if you discern a pattern. Are the events that you successfully predicted of a similar nature? The fact that you were able to predict them indicates that they were particularly important to you—in making your predictions, you were indicating that you were consciously aware of your desire for those events to happen. Why did you attract them to you; why were they attractive to you? Why are they significant to you? What are the beliefs involved?

As you continue to write down and check on your predictions, more than likely you will become aware of times when you do this predicting automatically. You may remember having "had a feeling" something was going to happen, and it did. Ask yourself: why did you have that feeling? What was the belief behind it? By becoming aware of this process of attracting probable events to your field of experience, you will gain greater understanding of why you create the reality you do, and how you can take a more conscious role in that process.

25

Clues
from the Past

Your present beliefs structure the memories which will parade
before you now—and what you remember will then seem to justify
the beliefs.

When you are trying to alter your beliefs, look through your past
with the new conceptions in mind. If you are ill, remember when
you were not [*The Nature of Personal Reality*, pp. 345–6].

In creating our reality, the past is a rich repository of events we can draw
from. As a matter of fact, we do this all the time, automatically making
decisions *now* based on our remembrance of past events. We may decide, say,
not to apply for a certain job because we didn't do well at a similar job in the past,
or because in the past we were turned down for such a job because we weren't
considered qualified. What we decide to do now is influenced by what we
remember as happening in the past.

But, as we have seen, time does not exist in Framework 2 where events
originate. Past, present and future are all happening *now*, and constantly
influencing one another. Thus you could just as easily say that what we decide to
do now influences what happens in the past. In any case, if we draw on the past
to influence our present and future—which we can indeed do—then it seems
much wiser to choose as our influence beneficial memories rather than detrimental ones. For the past contains triumphs as well as failures, joy as well as sorrow.
If we make an effort, we can always come up with "good" memories as well as
"bad" ones.

As we saw in the memory refresher exercise, we can draw on past
"highs" when we're feeling down and need to replenish our energy.
Similarly, we can look to the past for "clues" in understanding our present
and planning for the future. That is what this exercise will be concerned with.
The first part deals with finding clues to your present situation, and the
second part with using these clues as guidelines for the future.

Part One _____

Turn back to what you wrote in your journal for the Inventory of Successes
exercise, and for this exercise, select three or four of the successes you listed

there which are ones you want to continue to improve on. Perhaps you have gained a certain amount of skill at doing something and want to increase that skill. Or maybe you accumulated a certain amount of money and want to accumulate more.

Now, in your journal write down the first present success, and then trace the development of that achievement in the past. When is the first time you can remember having some success in that area? What events happened along the way to reinforce that first achievement? Did you "just happen" to meet certain people who were helpful to you? Did you "just happen" to pick up a book or a newspaper and read something that gave you beliefs that helped steer you in the right direction? Think of all the influences you can—beliefs you gained and actions you took—that led up to your present stage of development in that area.

Go through the same procedure with each of the other achievements you have chosen.

Part Two

Now write about the future *as if* it were the present. Pretend you are a future self, writing in your journal about influences leading to your present successes. Date the journal entry five years from now, and begin your chronicle with the present date. Recount the influences that have been responsible for your present outstanding achievement in the areas you focused on in the first part of the exercise. You saw what influenced your development in the past; now use these "clues" to project that development on into the future. What new steps will you "just happen" to take that will lead to even greater success in each of those areas? Be playful in doing this, and exaggerate as much as you want, but at the same time do include influences and actions that you really do believe could happen.

Read this account every now and again and see how you're doing at creating that reality for yourself.

26

The Road
Not Taken

If you find a line of development that you now wish you had pursued, but had not, then think deeply about the ways in which those activities could now fit into the framework of your officially-accepted life. Such musing, with desire—backed up by common sense—can bring about intersection points in probabilities that cause a fresh realignment of the deeper elements of the psyche. In such ways, probable events can be attracted to your present living situation [*The "Unknown" Reality,* Vol. 1, p. 180].

In the exercise on latent abilities, the idea of multipersonhood was introduced. The whole self consists of a nonphysical inner self and a multitude of physical selves or egos. Some of these selves exist in the same reality system but at different times. These are the so-called reincarnational selves (Seth prefers the term "simultaneous selves"). Other selves exist in a different system of reality—a probability system, where they live out ideas visualized in our reality, but not followed through on. Since ideas are basically mental acts, once they have been conceived in the mind, they exist as probabilities for physical materialization. If they are acted upon in this reality, they become actualized; if not, they continue their existence in the probability system, acted on by a probable self who springs into existence at the point of intersection when the decision is made, and verges off to follow in another reality the "road not taken" in this reality.

This means that for every action you visualized but did not take, there is a counterpart of yourself in a different system of reality, who did take that action and continued on from there to follow an independent path. What Seth is saying in the quoted passage is that under certain circumstances you can arrange it so that the path you are on now once again intersects with the path one of your probable selves is on, and the two of "you" can once again merge.

This exercise will explore that possibility—or, I should say, *probability.*

Think back to times in your life when you made major decisions which led to big changes in your life. Obvious examples are your decision of which college to go to, which job to choose, or whether or not to get married. Of these decisions, was there one that you have particularly regretted? Did everything seem to go wrong from that point on, or did you have a lot of second thoughts about it? Do you wish you had made another decision open to you at the time? If you cannot come up with any regrets of that sort, you can still do part of this exercise just to see what it feels like to explore probable realities, for as Seth says, "I do not like the phrase 'to advance,' yet in your terms 'to advance' as a consciousness is to become more and more aware of these other materializations of your own identity." If you *can* come up with a decision that you regretted, then plan on spending a lot of time on this exercise.

Go back to the time that you made that decision. Feel how you felt, visualize the environment and the circumstances that were then operating. Become the self that you were then. Now, envision yourself making, not the regretted decision, but the one you wish you had made. Feel the rush of excitement that one feels after making any life-changing decision, and set off on the path which following that action puts you on. Clearly envision all the new probable actions that arise as a result of that decision. See yourself following that path and taking advantage of all the opportunities that come up along the way. Now, while you are doing this, allow some of your awareness still to be connected with your present situation, with your present path, and envision these two paths coming back together at some point along the way. What actions can you take on that probable path that would be beneficial and at the same time not lead you too far astray from where you are now? What actions can you take in "real" life that would bring your path closer to the probable path you are envisioning?

This exercise requires solitude and intense concentration and determination. Do it several times, and write any insights you get from it in your journal. After several tries, you may be able to align the two paths.

27

Belief Assignment #5

> If you look about you at your relatives, friends, acquaintances, and business associates, you will also see what kind of a person you are, for you are drawn to them as they are drawn to you, through very basic inner similarities [*Seth Speaks*, p. 194].

In this belief assignment, you are going to examine your own beliefs through examining the beliefs of those people you have chosen to include in your life in some way. In your journal, make a list of the significant people in your life. In some cases these may not be people you are particularly close to, but who nonetheless have affected your life in some way, such as employers or employees, a landlord, or even a famous person you've never met but feel drawn to.

Now, for each person on the list, see if you can come up with several beliefs characteristic of that person, which are ones you also hold. Think of what you do to support one another in these beliefs. What is it you each say or do to strengthen these common beliefs?

Now think of some of the beliefs you are working on—ones that you want to see manifested in your reality. Do you know anyone now who has similar beliefs? Are you drawn toward people who have manifested these beliefs that you are working on?

Go on to consider what effects it would have on your relationship with different people on your list if you changed certain beliefs. Would you want this to happen? Do you have any beliefs you would like to change, except that you would lose the support of some of these people?

Think also of people who used to be your associates but no longer are. What beliefs did you have in common when you were associates? Do you both still have these beliefs, or did one of you change? Have you ever sought out the friendship of someone who didn't want to be friends with you, or vice versa? In either case, what beliefs do you think were operating on both sides?

28

Changing Beliefs by Substituting the Opposite

It is vital that you realize that you *are* working with beliefs in your mind. That the real work is done there in the mind—and not look for *immediate* physical results.

They will follow as *surely and certainly* as the "bad" results followed, and this must be a belief that the good results will come. But the real work is done in your mind. If you do the work, then you can rest assured of the results, but you must not check constantly for them [*The Nature of Personal Reality*, p. 73].

By this time, through doing these exercises you have no doubt uncovered a number of beliefs about yourself that you may not have been aware of before, or, if you were, didn't realize were limiting you. Now the question is, how to get rid of unwanted beliefs? Certainly recognizing their existence is a necessary first step, but then what? Can you just say "I hold that belief no more," and expect it to go away?

Well, perhaps you can—especially if you believe strongly that that will happen. But a more powerful method of changing a belief is by replacing it with another belief. By focusing your energy on a belief that leads to quite a different reality than the one your current belief does, you leave no energy for the current belief. And if you keep doing this, after a time the new belief will materialize, and thus become a part of your "official" reality. You can then concentrate on *another* belief you want materialized.

In our minds, we all have many beliefs that we have not acted upon, but lie latent and ready to be used. For instance, if you have an actively-expressed belief that you are poor, you also have a belief lying latent that you live in abundance—for a belief in poverty *presupposes* that another, happier state exists, of which you are deprived. Thus, for every "bad" active belief you have, there is a "good" belief lying latent and ready to be activated. And just by diverting your attention from the negative belief to the positive one, you begin to shift the balance of power to the other side.

In changing your beliefs, another thing to remember is that emotion and imagination are closely allied with beliefs and serve to strengthen them.

People tend to think that emotions and imagination *cause* beliefs, but that is not the case. Emotions rise out of belief, and so does the imagination. When you change a belief, you will find that your emotions change and that your imagination goes on to other things, for their source—the belief behind them—has changed. At the same time, emotions and imagination can be employed to strengthen the formation of a new belief in your mind.

Now, in changing a belief by substituting the opposite, the first step is to admit that you have a certain belief. The point is *not* to ignore or deny the old belief, for that only leads to a sense of powerlessness as the unexpressed emotions arising out of that belief build up inside. Instead, accept the belief *as* a belief that you currently have about your reality and realize that it is not a fact about reality itself. Then say to yourself, "I am going to pretend for a while that I have quite the opposite point of view. This can have nothing but good results." Then vividly imagine yourself in the opposite situation. If you are sick, imagine yourself well; if you are poor, imagine yourself rich. For that period of time, *be* the well person, *be* the rich person, and let your emotions and imagination flow. See yourself glowing with exuberant health; see and feel yourself joyfully spending money. Follow this by the point of power exercise, and see yourself creating this reality for yourself from your point of power in the present. Then let go of it, and *know* that physical results will follow eventually, and that you don't have to keep checking to see if they are. Do one small thing each day in keeping with your new belief. If you are sick in bed, get up out of bed for a few minutes. If you think yourself poor, spend money on some small frivolous thing.

In doing such an exercise, your imagination will often lead you into discovering other beliefs that you were not aware of. By imagining yourself in the opposite situation from the one you are in, you may run up against resistances to that state that you didn't know you had. For instance, you may discover that you resist being wealthy because you believe there is too much responsibility connected with it. This discovery may lead you to a cluster of beliefs you have about responsibility that may be standing in the way of many accomplishments. You can then employ the same strategy in working on these beliefs.

29

Your Ideal Self

As lovers can see the "ideal" in their beloved and yet be well aware of certain inadequacies, certain deviations from the ideal, so can you, loving yourself, realize that what you think of as imperfect are gropings toward a more complete becoming [*The Nature of Personal Reality*, p. 498].

Seth continually stresses the importance of self-acceptance. Basically, we are all idealists. Our inborn impetus toward value fulfillment, toward the realization of all our potentialities, toward the fulfillment of our ideal psychological pattern, constantly propels us to strive toward the "betterment" of ourselves. We take courses on improving our memories or investing in real estate or cooking Japanese recipes; we read all the self-help books we can get our hands on; we go to marriage counselors, assertiveness training workshops, and health spas.

Though this constant urge to improve upon ourselves, to become more complete, has a strong natural basis, in our society it has become perverted and misused. Instead of taking pleasure in our learning and enjoying the creativity of our changing selves, we compare ourselves to others and feel lacking. Or we compare ourselves to an idealized version of ourselves and feel guilty for not living up to our potential. We have come to focus so intently on the product out there—that "finished" self we some day hope to be—that we no longer enjoy the process of *becoming* that self. Before any self-improvement efforts will be effective, it is very important that we accept and affirm the self we are *right now*. For otherwise, we will never be satisfied, we will always be putting ourselves down, pointing out to ourselves how much better other people do in whatever area we are hoping to improve, and focusing on what we "ought" to be doing. If we can just accept who we are here and now, then we can love ourselves and, from that vantage point, can see the ideal in ourselves. Then, if we become aware of certain inadequacies or deviations, we can welcome them, as indications of ways we *can* become more complete in our pursuit of the ideal.

This exercise should be done in the spirit of joyous self-exploration and discovery. For its purpose will be to find out what your idealized version of yourself is through examining the "gropings" you are presently going through. By looking at what you are *not* in your beliefs, you will discover what you think you *are* —what your ideal psychological pattern is, that pattern in Framework 2 which the inner self is eternally nudging you into fulfilling.

In your journal, make a list of all your failings. What you do wrong or imperfectly, what you lack, what you cannot do. Be playful about this, realizing it is your *beliefs* about yourself that you are writing down, and that there are really no limits to yourself. All you need do is change your beliefs, and your reality will change with them. Think of incidents in which you did something or behaved in a way that you are ashamed of. Make a long list of your "defects."

Now examine this list to see what it says about your idealized notion of yourself. For example, if one of the things you said about yourself is that you talk too much, what does this say about your "ideal" self—that your ideal person is one who listens to what others say? Who doesn't feel the need to show off? Go through your list by examining traits you are critical of, and see if you can come up with a list of characteristics that you feel are the ideal ones for yourself. Whenever you are critical, it is because you have failed to live up to your unique psychological pattern.

Now write a description of this ideal self, in the third person, as if you were a good friend of this character. What does this person do and say? What kind of life does he or she have? Again, be playful, realizing this ideal is constantly changing, not set in concrete.

As a final step in this exercise, reflect on the *impulses* you receive that impel you toward becoming this idealized person. Think of a few recent cases in which you felt an impulse to do something, and see it in the light of your ideal psychological pattern, your ideal self. Realize what an idealist you are.

30

Rewriting the Past

> You can theoretically alter your own past as you know it, for time is no more something divorced from you than probabilities are.
>
> The past existed in multitudinous ways. You only experienced one probable past. By changing this past in your mind, now, in your present, you can change not only its nature but its effect, and not only upon yourself but upon others [*Seth Speaks*, p. 262].

As you have discovered by now, there are many facets to creating your own reality, and thus many different approaches. Simply being aware of your power is one approach to reality-creating. Becoming conscious of your impulses is another way of making the most of your reality-creating potential. Another approach is to examine your beliefs. Another is to affirm yourself. Another is to use a dialogue, and so on.

Several exercises have focussed on working with the past as a tool in creating your present reality. The memory-refresher exercise, for instance, showed you how to renew and refresh yourself in the present by using the energy generated by pleasant memories of the past. In another exercise you saw that by "meeting" past selves and giving them encouragement, you create a more positive present reality for yourself. Another exercise had you examining past successes and seeing how they contributed to your present situation. Following that was an exercise in which you explored a road not taken with the goal of bringing that road back to an intersection with your present one.

This exercise will give you yet another way of using the past in creating present reality. It is similar to Exercise 28, in which you substituted a present positive belief for the opposite, negative one. Except that in this exercise you will be substituting one past incident for another.

Try to recall an event in the past that was upsetting to you; an event you feel upset about when you recall it. It may have been something that you did, or something that someone else did. It may be that you felt depressed and powerless, or that you exploded in rage. You may have behaved in a way you have never understood, or you may understand very well why you behaved that way. In any case, it should be an incident that you still feel upset with yourself about.

Now, in your journal, go back to the time just before that incident occurred. Describe the scene in detail—the setting, the characters, the emotional atmosphere. Then go on to describe what happened, but instead of using the incident you remember, substitute one with an entirely different outcome. Something very positive and affirming. Write in as great detail as possible what was said, what the reactions were, the feeling of resolution of what might otherwise have been an unfortunate outcome. As you write, see the facial expressions, hear the tones of voice, sense your impulses and your emotions. Make it real.

Read this over many times on different occasions, and each time feel yourself living the scene as you have written it. As Seth says, it is not being self-deluding to tell yourself that another more positive event happened in place of the one you remember. Thoughts about the past *are* actions in the past, and thus, by thinking of this new past action, you automatically make it a probable event in the past. It may not have been the one you "officially" experienced, the one you chose to perceive in your "real" past, but it *is* a probable event, and thus will have its effect on you, and on the other people who were involved in the incident—if they choose to accept your new version.

There is no end to the interactions constantly taking place between past, present, and future. Seth mentions, for instance, that a sudden, intense belief in health can actually "reverse" a long-standing disease. New cellular memories replace old ones in the body, so that its past will be in harmony with its present. This means that the past can learn from the present, as well as the other way around.

These many different approaches to changing your beliefs support and reinforce one another, and bring into play emotions, imagination, and intellect.

31

Secrets

> I suggest now that when I am finished, for a preliminary starter,
> each of you tell a secret [*Conversations with Seth*, Vol. 1, p. 86].

In one of Jane's regular ESP classes, Seth made the assignment that everyone tell a secret about themselves. He had been talking to the class about being honest, and said they needed to acknowledge their feelings so that they could direct that emotional energy in the way they wished.

> Now we have spoken in terms that you could understand—the
> nature of your world and reality as you know it. But you have not
> taken the stuff of reality into your hearts and understood it, and
> this is what you must now begin to learn to do. In other words, you
> must accept the emotional self, not superficially, not idealistically,
> but as it now exists; the reality of what you are *now* —and then you
> can begin to work with what you are and what you have
> [*Conversations with Seth*, Vol. 1, p. 86].

He then suggested that they tell a secret about themselves to the other class members. This could be a secret that they had told to close friends or their mate, but which they would not want the world at large to know. This, he said, would be "a preliminary step in expressing honesty" and also in communicating heretofore-hidden experiences and feelings.

Everyone in class seemed to be taken aback by this assignment, according to Sue Watkins, who described the session in *Conversations with Seth*. Each person would blurt out his or her secret with great trepidation, only to discover that the others were not at all shocked by the disclosure. Sue stammeringly confessed to having once hit her pet dog with a stick. This got little reaction from the audience. Another class member then haltingly told of hating his elderly father who lived with him. Sue said she felt like sneering at him. She couldn't see what a big deal *that* was when compared to having hit one's dog with a stick. Now there was a big deal! Thus the class learned that what are significant and shameful acts to *you* may not seem significant or shameful to anyone else. Such behavior affects you adversely only because of your *belief* in its negativity.

If you can do this exercise with a friend, that would be best. But if not, write a script of an imaginary ESP class in which you and the others tell secrets about yourselves. While writing this, see if you can maintain two viewpoints—the viewpoint of an objective observer, and the viewpoint of your ego telling the secret. See if you can feel the strong emotion of shame while telling the secret, and also view the emotion (and the stimulus behind it) as no big deal, just a part of the living process.

As a follow-up to this, write down any other secrets you can think of about yourself. Ask yourself: would anyone else really think they are as negative as you do? Make it a point to start revealing these things about yourself to others, thereby releasing the emotional charge behind them. You will feel better in being honest with others—and relieved to find that people, rather than thinking worse of you because they know your secret, will instead feel more positive toward you for being open.

Continue to be on the lookout for secrets you hold about yourself, for often you will keep secrets even from yourself. Since these secrets block the revelation of important beliefs that are holding you back in some way, they are the most damaging ones of all. Seth told the class,

> ... You should realize the vitality that is distorted in these deep charges that you often carry within you, for these deny you the use of your own energy. They literally tie you up in knots [*Conversations with Seth*, Vol. 1, p. 91].

32

Your Personal Myth

Myth-making is a natural psychic characteristic, a psychic element that combines with other such elements to form a mythical representation of inner reality. That representation is then used as a model upon which your civilizations are organized, and also as a perceptual tool through whose lens you interpret the private events of your life... [*The Individual and The Nature of Mass Events,* p. 89].

We invent myths in order to answer questions we have about the nature of reality. Seth uses the example of people caught in a natural disaster. Depending on their beliefs, they might ask themselves whether God caused the disaster to wreak vengeance on them for some wrongdoing. Or if they are scientifically-oriented, they might ask how technology could be improved so as to better predict such disasters and save lives. Dramatic life-threatening situations will always bring to mind such questions about the nature of reality and our connection with nature, the universe, and God. These questions lead to the development of myths, which are then used as guiding principles in life.

Because our society distrusts anything that smacks of the "mystical" or "irrational," we call our myths facts and accept them as basic rules of existence. Losing their flexibility and symbolic power, the myths become invisible constraints, programming our lives rather than guiding them. Both Christianity and science are mythical in nature, though it would be most difficult for a scientist to perceive the mythical characteristics of science— while he or she might be quite willing to ascribe such characteristics to Christianity, or for the Christian to see his or her religion as based on myth— though perhaps seeing science in that light. In any case, we are to some extent prevented from recognizing the "magical" ever-changing nature of reality because of our conversion of myths into "facts." This limits us.

In doing this exercise, you will get re-acquainted with the myth-making propensities you exercised so freely as a child, and also have the experience of creating your own personal myth, in which you supply your own symbolic explanation of the nature of reality and of your position within it. This should lead to some insights about your deepest beliefs.

As a preliminary to this exercise, mull over in your mind the myths, legends, and tales that you are familiar with. Focus on the main characters in these stories—Cinderella, Adam and Eve, Ulysses, and so on. Recall the conflicts these characters had, the obstacles in their paths, their allies and opponents and their final fate. This will give you a feel for the myth-making medium. Now think of a pivotal event in your life, a time when you came up against some elemental forces in your nature, or in Nature outside yourself. As you recall the event, try to see its mythical qualities, to see what it has in common with myths. Ask yourself questions such as "Why did this happen to me?" "What forces were at work behind the scenes here?" "What inner reality did these three-dimensional characters (or actions) represent?" "How can I represent this struggle mythically?"

Then write your own personal myth in your journal. Don't force the symbols. Let them arise naturally out of your impulses. Don't try to "make sense" or be rational. Just write what comes to mind, and then see what you have. Go over the myth in the same way you do dreams, doing free associations of the images until the meaning becomes clear to you. Write down any new beliefs you discovered. Are they limiting to you?

33

Belief Assignment
#6

You are in physical existence to learn and understand that your energy, translated into feelings, thoughts and emotions, causes *all* experience. *There are no exceptions.*

Once you understand this, you have only to learn to examine the nature of your beliefs, for these will automatically cause you to feel and think in certain fashions. Your emotions follow your beliefs. It is not the other way around.

I would like you to recognize your own beliefs in several areas. You must realize that any idea you accept as *truth* is a belief that *you* hold. You must then take the next step and say, "It is not necessarily true, even though I believe it." You will, I hope, learn to disregard all beliefs that imply *basic* limitations [*The Nature of Personal Reality*, p. 26].

This is a modified version of a belief assignment that Seth gave in Jane's ESP class.

In your journal, write down your beliefs about responsibility. What is the nature of responsibility? How do you feel about responsibility? What do you believe you are responsible for? Now, of these responsibilities, are there some that you enjoy and others you don't? Focus on the ones you don't enjoy. How well do you do tasks that you feel responsible for, but don't enjoy?

Now go on to the idea of fun. What is fun to do? How do you feel about having fun? Do you "allow" yourself to do fun-loving things? Are there some fun-loving things that you don't feel are "legitimate" for you to do? When you do a task because it is fun, how well do you do it? Do you do tasks *better* when you enjoy them than when you do them because you feel responsible for them? If so, how can you make responsibility more fun? When he assigned this exercise, Seth said:

> I use the word *fun* purposely, because when I use the word *joy*, you can hide behind it, and think, in what you think of as high spiritual terms, for *joy* sounds spiritual and *fun* does not! [*Conversations with Seth*, Vol. 1, p. 200].

34

Memory Refresher #2

In some underground of sensation...the buried evidences of stimuli and reaction experienced during those numberless "past" afternoons still exist. Some of those memories will certainly be played back, to affect what you think of as your current experience.... Your conscious thoughts and habits regulate which of them will intermix into the maelstrom of the present.... Past events do not intrude...unless they are beckoned by the conscious expectations and thoughts that exist within your mind. Those unconscious memories will be activated according to your current beliefs. You will be replenished and renewed as your thoughts motivate joyful body sensations and physical events, or you will be depressed as you bring into your awareness unpleasant past body happenings.... If you pursue...sorrowful thoughts persistently, you are reactivating that body condition. Think of one of the most pleasant events...and the reverse will be true.... Remember, these mental associations are living things. They are formations of energy assembled into invisible structures [*The Nature of Personal Reality*, pp. 147, 153].

As with the previous memory refresher exercise, do not try to do all of the items in this exercise in one time period. Fifteen to twenty minutes a day is about the right time to spend on these. Otherwise they may lose their effect. For each item, close your eyes and experience the incident. Project yourself into it. Notice the colors and sensations. Savor them. Then let the scene end, and feel the effect on your body now. Sense the energy surging through you. Feel yourself in the future with this energetic feel. Any time you are feeling low, refer to this exercise, find an item that particularly exhilarated you, and go through this same procedure with it, to replenish and renew yourself.

Remember a time when:

- you felt a sense of accomplishment
- you made someone happy
- you were glad to be alive

- you held someone close
- time stopped
- you were chosen by someone
- you had it out with someone and felt better
- you felt beautiful
- you saw into someone's soul
- you felt free
- your friends showed their love for you
- someone understood you
- you realized how capable you are
- you knew for sure that you create your own reality
- you sat in the warm sun
- you solved a problem
- you *knew* everything always works out
- someone trusted you
- you changed your behavior
- you stuck to your guns
- your joy knew no bounds
- you realized you had done something important
- you knew you were strong
- someone spoke to you with respect
- you squished mud between your toes
- your fears were unfounded
- you discovered you really mattered to someone
- you felt skillful
- you surrendered
- you were of real help to someone

35

Devil's Advocate

Many quite limiting ideas will pass without scrutiny under the guise of goodness. You may feel quite virtuous, for example, in hating evil, or what seems to you to be evil; but if you find yourself concentrating upon either hatred or evil, you are creating it. If you are poor you may feel quite self-righteous in your financial condition, looking with scorn upon those who are wealthy, telling yourself that money is wrong and so reinforcing the condition of poverty.... If you are ill, you may find yourself dwelling upon the misery of your condition, and bitterly envying those who are healthy, bemoaning your state—and therefore perpetuating it through your thoughts.... Hatred of war will not bring peace—another example. Only love of peace will bring those conditions [*The Nature of Personal Reality*, p. 37].

Reality-creating can be a tricky business. We realize we create it through our beliefs, and we know that our beliefs are conscious. But that still doesn't keep a lot of them from escaping our notice. They have become so familiar to us that we don't even realize they are beliefs. Or, if we recognize them, they seem to be "good," constructive beliefs, so we don't examine them further. And yet it is these very beliefs—the ones we take for granted and the ones we consider to be positive—that can cause us the most difficulty.

In this exercise, you are going to play the devil's advocate. You are going to take the unpopular, "evil" point of view and see what you can do to defend it. In many cases you will not be able to, or not want to. But in some cases you may find that what you have considered to be positive, unlimiting beliefs are really quite limiting. Seth's example of hatred of war is a case in point. War is so "obviously" evil, who wouldn't hate it? And yet through focussing our energy on the idea of war, we give it reality and power.

In your journal, make a list of all the beliefs you can think of that you consider to be beneficial, unlimiting, ideas to live by, such as "Honesty is the best policy," or "Smoking is dangerous to your health." Include cliches and aphorisms, for these are particularly invisible—they "go without saying."

Now, playing the devil's advocate, go down this list and see if you can "disprove" each of these ideas. Are there any disadvantages or limitations to believing it? Could having such a belief cause you or anybody else harm? What underlying assumptions is the belief based on? For instance, in the statement "Smoking is dangerous to your health," an underlying assumption is that dangers to your health exist. Is this assumption, to you, "an idea to live by"? Or is it limiting? For each idea that you found flaws in, see if you can restate it so that it is *un*limiting.

36

Belief Assignment #7

If you allow yourself to be more and more aware of your own beliefs, you can work with them. It is silly to try to fight what you think of as negative beliefs, or to be frightened of them. *They are not mysterious.* You may find that many served good purposes at one time, but that they have simply been overemphasized. They may need to be restructured rather than denied.... Some beliefs may work very positively for you for certain periods of your life. Because you have not *examined* them, however, you may carry them long after they have served their purpose, and now they may work against you.... For example, many of the young believe at one time or another that their parents are omnipotent—a very handy belief that gives children a sense of security. Grown into adolescent years, the same offspring are then shocked to discover their parents to be quite human and fallible, and another conviction often takes over: a belief in the inadequacy and inferiority of the older generations, and in the rigidity and callousness of those who run the world.... If at the age of forty you still believe in the infallibility of your parents, then you hold that idea way beyond its advantageous state for you.... If you are fifty and still convinced that the older generations are rigid...then you are...setting up negative suggestions for yourself [*The Nature of Personal Reality*, pp. 550–51].

As Seth says, we often carry with us beliefs that were once useful to us in one way or another, but which now hold us back. For this belief assignment, you will be examining beliefs in terms of how useful they are to you *at this time.* Begin by going back to your childhood, and think of the beliefs you had. Examining your parents' beliefs will give you some ideas. Write these down in your journal. Do you still have any of these beliefs? If you do, are they still useful to you? What purpose do they serve?

Go on into your adolescence and examine the beliefs you had at the time. What did you and your peers think about your role in the world? What were your attitudes toward parents, toward authority? Write these down and examine them. How many of these beliefs do you still hold? Are they useful to you, or limiting?

Go on into your twenties and examine those beliefs. Which of those do your still have? Are *they* useful? And so on. When you are finished, decide what you are going to do about your outdated beliefs.

37

Healing
Through Sound

When your body and mind are working together then the relationship between the two goes smoothly, and their natural therapeutic systems place you in a state of health and grace.... It is because you do not trust your own basic therapeutic nature...that you run to so many therapies that originate from without the self [*The Nature of Personal Reality*, pp. 216–7].

Animals rely totally on their instinct to maintain their bodies and tell them what actions to take. There is no separation between "parts" of their mind. But we create our reality differently. Conscious thought plays an important role in directing unconscious activities. In evaluating our experience and deciding whether or not to change it, we rely on *both* conscious and unconscious signals. In this sense, we are more responsible for our health and welfare than animals are—which may be a source of difficulty. We want to "do something" about a physical symptom, for instance, and are unwilling—or afraid—to wait and see what develops. We just do not trust our bodies as a self-regulating system, and feel we must take responsibility for setting them aright. And so we take pills, visit a doctor, or make an appointment with a psychiatrist. Because we *are* conscious, we are aware of our responsibility in creating our own reality, and this sense of responsibility prevents us from trusting in our own therapeutic nature. Yet we *are* our own best therapists, because only we can know for sure when we are experiencing inner harmony.

A state of grace exists when mind, body, and psyche are in perfect balance; when we are consciously aware of a biological and psychic unity within and in relationship to the universe. This state of physical, mental, and psychic harmony can be triggered by the smallest events. Smelling a rose can evoke joy and the thought of your beloved. Finely attuned to the senses, our conscious mind has the capacity to interpret events in a multitude of ways—something the animals cannot do. We can consciously use our senses, then, to call forth the power and strength of our inner reality and bring about the sense of unity that is, or should be, the goal of all therapy.

The power of music as a natural form of therapy is well-known, though the reason for its effectiveness has not always been recognized. Seth gives this explanation:

You perceive [your bodies] as objects, with bulk, composed of bone and flesh. They also have "structures" of sound...connected with the physical image that you know. Any physical disabilities will show themselves in these other "structures" initially.

The sound...patterns give strength and vitality to the physical form that you recognize.... The sounds contain with them a built-in impetus toward energy and well-being.... Music is an exterior representation, and an excellent one, of the life-giving inner sounds that act therapeutically within your body all the time. The music is a conscious reminder of those deeper inner rhythms.... Listening to music that you like will often bring images into your mind that show you your conscious beliefs in different forms [*The Nature of Personal Reality*, pp. 105, 106, 217].

Listening to music, then, helps us to unite the conscious mind with the body and the deeper structures of our being—with the feeling-tones of energy that sing our identity to the world.

This exercise is so enjoyable and easy to do that it may not seem like an "exercise" at all. But doing it every day will improve your overall sense of well-being and harmony. Simply put aside a half an hour a day and listen to music. Choose a time when you will most likely not be interrupted. Lie down on a couch or on cushions on the floor, breathe deeply, and feel yourself relaxing as the music flows into you.

It is best to choose records or tapes that you haven't listened to a lot, so that you won't be anticipating the sounds that are coming, and will be giving your full attention to each note as it is played. With your eyes closed, let the thoughts come into your mind and pass by. Don't hold onto any ideas. Let images come in response to the music, without trying to interpret them. Be aware of the feelings that go with the thoughts. Feel the sounds resonating deep within the cells of your body and sense the sound waves radiating outward from your body and becoming part of the vibrations of the universe. Totally experience the music.

When it is over, quickly write down in your journal any insights you may have had during the experience, while they are still fresh in your mind. Become more aware of the everyday sounds around you; particularly the sounds of nature—the birds chirping, wind in the trees, rain on the roof, the sound of the sea. Just by understanding the therapeutic nature of sounds, your listening will be enhanced.

38

Imagine

Through training, many adults have been taught that the imagination itself is suspicious. Such attitudes not only drastically impede any artistic creativity, but the imaginative creativity necessary to deal with the nature of physical events themselves [*The Nature of The Psyche,* p. 176].

As Seth says, it isn't only artists who need to use their imagination; everyone does, simply to deal with ordinary reality. Here is an exercise that will get you to stretch your imagination.

Seth mentions that children's play is often involved with manipulation in time, while adult's games are concerned with manipulations in space. So see if you can re-train your mind to work like a child's, whose creativity knows no bounds. Imagine yourself in the same space you are now in, but at a time in the distant past. Write in your journal your impressions of this place as it was many centuries ago. What was the terrain like then? What kind of shelters were there? What were the people like? How were they dressed?

Now imagine this same place again, but many centuries into the distant future. What do you see now? Describe it in detail in your journal.

You can do similar tricks with your imagination any time. When you are on a walk, for instance, imagine what the area you are passing was like ten years before, or what it will be like ten years in the future. Or imagine what the trees you are looking at now looked like a season or two ago, and what they will look like in the coming season. Exercises like these will give you a perspective on the present that is quite valuable. We tend to perceive events as fixed in time, and need to get a sense of their fluidity. By actively imagining a space you are in as it appears in different time frames, you can develop a sense of this fluidity; of the ever-changing nature of reality.

39

The Pendulum

The pendulum would be a method of allowing you to view conscious material that is not structured to recognized beliefs [*The Nature of Personal Reality*, p. 70].

Yet another way of uncovering beliefs you are not aware of is to use the "pendulum." This is an old technique which Robert Butts, Jane's husband, has used successfully to uncover the reasons behind various phenomena in his life.

You make a pendulum by suspending a small but heavy object like a rock or a lead sinker from a string. Holding the string between the thumb and forefinger, you let the pendulum hang free. Then you ask questions that can be answered with either "yes" or "no" and, holding your hand perfectly still, wait for the "reply." Almost imperceptibly at first, but with ever increasing momentum, the pendulum will begin to swing, as your muscles respond "involuntarily" to the question.

Before you ask your question, decide on how to interpret the different motions of the pendulum. You may decide to use a back-and-forth swing, for instance, for your "yes" answers, and a side-to-side swing for "no." A circular motion you can use for "That question is unanswerable at this time," leaving it up to your inner self to decide whether getting the information you seek is in your best interests.

A disadvantage to this method, of course, is that you can *only* ask yes/no questions. But you can ask as many as you want, and thus, by the process of elimination, slowly zero in on fruitful areas. For instance, you may want to discover the reasons behind a vague feeling of depression that you cannot connect with any past experience. You might begin with general questions like "Is this feeling related to some specific event in my past?" If the pendulum signals "yes," then you can begin to ask it about events that come to mind. But if it says "no," then you can ask it whether the feeling is related to some anticipated event in the future. If it says "no," that means no specific event, in either the past or future is causing the feeling. You can then go on to ask if the feeling has to do with a series of events, or with a dream, or with a belief—and so on.

It is best to write down the questions before you ask them, and to record the answers you get. The pendulum will take questions very literally, so that often the mere change of a word or two in the question will change the answer you get.

Be careful not to "influence" your answers, especially when you are asking questions that you *want* certain answers to. If you find you are getting exactly the answers you had been hoping for every time, this may mean that you are putting "body English" on them. This in itself will tell you something about your feelings and the beliefs behind them, but it may not uncover some of the beliefs causing the situation you're asking about. When you get an answer that you did not expect or want, at least you can be sure that it is not coming from the ego, but from the inner self.

This is a good method to use in checking out beliefs that you suspect are intellectual assumptions based on what you "ought" to think. You can simply ask, "Do I really believe such and such?" and the pendulum will give you a straight answer. Don't rely on the pendulum, though, to make predictions for you: "Will it rain on Saturday?" or "Will I find a lover within a month?" For one thing, asking such questions tends to subvert your faith in the benevolence of Framework 2. Also, as we have seen, the future is fluid and ever-changing, so the pendulum can tell you only the likelihood of something occurring. And if that likelihood is an unfortunate one, you may draw it to you by the expectations set up by the answer, rather than making the effort to bring about a more fortunate outcome. The best use of the pendulum is in discovering beliefs, not in making decisions.

40

Belief Assignment
#8

As you examine the contents of your conscious mind, it may seem
to you that you hold so many different beliefs at different times that
you cannot correlate them. They will, however, form into clear
patterns. You will find a group of core beliefs about which others
gather.... They *are* consciously available. You can find them
through... working from your feelings or by beginning with the
beliefs that become most readily available.... As you examine your
ideas, you will discover that even some apparently contradictory ones
have similarities, and these resemblances may be used to bridge the
gaps between beliefs—even those that seem to be the most diverse.
These aspects will themselves emerge as bridge beliefs.... When you
discover what they are, you will find a point of unity within yourself
from which you can, with some detachment, view your other systems
of belief.... Various core beliefs, not well assimilated, will give you
conflicting self-images.... Usually *exaggerated* opposing emotions
will also be apparent. Once you understand this, it is not difficult to
look at your beliefs, to identify these, and to find a bridge to unite the
seeming contradictions [*The Nature of Personal Reality*, pp. 254–6].

Seth's discussion of bridge beliefs arose out of an experience Jane Roberts had
in which she discovered a bridge belief of hers which reconciled two
conflicting core beliefs she had about herself. One core belief was that she was
a writer. She viewed her world of experience through this perspective of
herself as a writer, encouraged impulses that furthered this image of herself,
and discouraged ones that did not.

   Then, when her psychic experiences began to occur, Jane gained
another core belief: that she was a psychic. Accordingly, she began to
encourage impulses toward psychic activity. But a conflict soon developed:
Jane found herself resistant to any psychic activities that involved writing. In
trying to get its experiences down on paper, Jane's psychic self always met
with resistance from Jane's "writer" self. The psychic self wasn't allowed to
write during Jane's usual five-hour writing day, and had to find other times to
do so.

   At the same time, Jane found that her writer self was more and more
restricted in the material it could use, for topics that smacked of "psychic"

things were not "proper" material for a writer to use. To the writer self, who was accustomed to writing fiction and poetry, writing about psychic experiences was not "real" writing.

So Jane's writer self kept feeling more restricted, jealously guarding its "writer" status. In the meantime, the psychic self went blithely on its way turning out page after page of writing, unbothered by the judgments of the writer self. Jane found that she was having conversations between the two of them in her head, until one day she realized: both the writing and psychic aspects of herself *were writers* —writers of different kinds, but both of them writers. This was the bridge belief that united the two selves in her mind, and resolved the conflict. She no longer held the two selves in opposition by thinking of one as a writer and the other one as not a writer. It was all right for both of them to write and use whatever material they wished.

For this eighth belief assignment, examine contradictory beliefs in yourself. For instance, you may find that you believe yourself to be very disciplined in some ways and lazy in others. You find your "disciplined" self being critical of your "lazy" self. Or perhaps you believe yourself to be a "woman" on the one hand and a "boss" on the other, and cannot reconcile the two because of your beliefs about how women should behave. Everyone has many such contradictory beliefs.

In your journal, make two columns with contradictory beliefs at the top; e.g., "I am disciplined" and "I am lazy." Under each heading, write down more specific beliefs that are implied by the general ones. For instance, under "I am disciplined" you might write "It is good to be disciplined." And under "I am lazy," "It is bad to be lazy." If you find it difficult to think of beliefs, think of traits that you would ascribe to that personality (e.g., efficient, productive; irresponsible, useless); or feelings you have about that self, or simply the actions or behavior of a self that believes that.

After you have made a list for each belief, see if you can find a common element that unites the two of them. In examining the behavior of your "disciplined" and "lazy" selves, for instance, you might find that both enjoy a routine; it's only that the lazy self likes to watch certain TV programs and read abed on Sunday mornings while the disciplined self does more "productive" things.

The point of this exercise, of course, is to reconcile conflicting beliefs about yourself so that you can allow both "sides" to exist without being critical or judgmental of one another. By finding a belief that both selves hold, you can bring them together, bridging the gap between seeming opposites. This defuses the conflict and lets you behave in ways that you had previously believed to be not permissible.

41

Five Years
from Now

Imagination...plays an important part in your subjective life, as it gives mobility to your beliefs. It is one of the motivating agencies that helps transform your beliefs into physical experience. It is vital therefore that you understand the interrelationship between ideas and imagination. In order to dislodge unsuitable beliefs and establish new ones, you must learn to use your imagination to move concepts in and out of your mind. The proper use of imagination can then propel ideas in the direction you desire [*The Nature of Personal Reality*, pp. 64–5].

Many of the exercises in this workbook have involved the use of imagination as a means of discovering beliefs, of changing beliefs and of propelling them into actualization. Imagination is one of the most powerful tools we can use in reality-creating. This exercise, another one utilizing imagination, will overlap with some of the previous exercises—as other exercises have—serving to lend support and strength to new beliefs and trends you want to get going.

In your journal, write a story about the you of five years from now. Describe your daily life in as much detail as possible including your house, your clothes, the food you eat. Envision your daily activities, your interactions with family, friends and associates, your work, your travels, your leisure-time activities. If in previous exercises you have been envisioning the development of a talent in the future, picture it developed now and picture yourself going through the motions you would go through in exercising this talent.

Look at the products that result from your efforts. If you have envisioned getting a further education, look at yourself five years from now with that education complete, and see how you use the fruits of that education. Include as much sensual detail as possible—sights, sounds, tastes, smells, textures. Be playful about this and let the images unfold from one another.

When you are finished, compare what you have written here with what you wrote for the "clues from the past" exercise where you wrote about yourself having developed certain skills in the future. How do these two scenarios compare? Have your beliefs changed since writing the first one? Do you feel you integrated the skills into your projected future here in a way that you didn't in the previous exercise?

42

Befriending
the Future You

Suppose you have a particular goal in mind as a youngster, toward which you work. Your intent, images, desires and determination form a psychic force that is projected out ahead of you, so to speak. You send the reality of yourself from your present into what you think of as the future.... Say that at a certain stage you have some decision to make and do not know which way to turn. You may sense that you are in danger of swerving from your purpose, yet for other reasons feel strongly inclined to do so. In a dream or in daydreaming, you may suddenly hear a voice, mentally, that tells you in no uncertain terms to go ahead with your initial intent...the self that you have projected into the future is sending you back encouragement from a probable reality that you still can create. That focused self operates from its *present*, however, and some day in your own future you may find yourself thinking nostalgically of a moment back in your past, when you were indecisive or irresolute, but took the proper course. You may think, "I am glad I did that," or "Knowing what I know now, how lucky I am that I made that decision." And in that moment you *are* the future self that "once" spoke encouragingly to the person of the past. The probable future has caught up with the practical present [*The Nature of Personal Reality*, pp. 495–6].

Earlier, in exercise #20, we talked about the idea of a single lifetime being a series of reincarnational existences. The self you were ten years ago is not the self you are now. You are who you are now because of the experiences you—or earlier versions of you—went through during your life, but because of those experiences, you have changed and are not the you who experienced them. Those earlier selves are very much like reincarnational selves; versions of you living in a different time frame.

We also saw how the concept of karma could apply *within* this lifetime as well as among lifetimes. Because of your choices in the past, you learned certain things and did not learn others. Today we are concerned with developing in the areas that we opened up for ourselves earlier and also in ridding ourselves of old behavior patterns that may be holding us back. Because time does not exist, all our earlier selves exist *now*, and we can influence them as they can influence us.

We can "go back" to those earlier selves and encourage them and replenish their energy in times of stress.

All of this applies to "future" selves as well as "past" selves. In our present we have projected ourselves into the future innummerable times. Whenever we have had a thought about ourselves in the future we have "created" a probable self who is living out that fantasy, for, as we have seen, our every thought is a reality, an action taken, which manifests either in our system of reality—if we choose to actualize it—or in another system of reality—a system of probabilities.

Reincarnational selves are closely related to probable selves. Reincarnational selves have their existence in this system of reality, but in different time frames from our point of view (but simultaneously from a Framework 2 point of view); probable selves have their existence in a different system of reality, the probability system. In our future—as in our past—there exist many probable selves. One of these will become the "you" of the future. This will be that probable self you choose to "become." That self then becomes actualized in this system of reality and thus a part of the reincarnational system, rather than the probable system.

We all have ideas of what we would like to become. In this workbook you have done a number of exercises exploring your potentialities, and in the power point of the present projecting yourself into the future. You have, through looking at your past efforts, seen the ideal psychological pattern you are striving toward in this lifetime. The ideal self, the one who comes closest to fulfilling that pattern, is a probable self now existing in your future. That self can become the actualized you of the present some day. (Of course, by becoming that self you will change it, as we have seen.)

The better "acquainted" you are with this future self, the more likely your paths will come together and merge in the future. This self can help you to make the choices that will lead you ever closer to its reality. Much as you gave encouragement to your earlier self, this self can encourage you and renew your energy when you need it. You will have the benefits of the wisdom of this self, who has already been through what you have yet to experience. There is a very wise self there in the future, the "you" who has fulfilled many of the values you are still looking to fulfill.

As a preliminary to doing this exercise, go back and read what you wrote for exercise #29 on your ideal self. Get a clear picture in your mind of this future self of yours. Now, in your journal, write an account of a meeting between this self and you. Describe the setting in detail, describe this being you have come to meet. Write a dialogue of what you say to one another. Ask this self to give you guidance along the way. Agree upon a signal you will use when you want to communicate with one another. Discuss some of the tasks you have ahead. Get whatever advice you can about doing them. Agree to meet regularly in your dreams. Say goodbye.

Read this scenario often. Continue your friendship with this future self.

43

Letting Go

Negative, distrustful, fearful, or degrading attitudes toward anyone work against the self.... You cannot escape your attitudes, for
they will form the nature of what you see.... What you see in
others is the materialization—the projection of what you *think* you
are...if others seem deceitful to you, it is because you deceive
yourself and then project it outward upon others...[*The Seth
Material,* pp. 178, 180].

To me, the most profound piece of advice ever given has been: fear not. All
things negative in our lives are caused by our fears. Insofar as we focus on our
fears, they will manifest themselves in one way or the other. As Seth says, you
get what you concentrate on. And all too often that translates out as, "you get
what you fear."

The emotions and the imagination, as we have seen, are the two most
powerful energy sources available to us. When we have a belief that arouses
fear in us, we give more power to that belief through that emotion. And our
imagination, always following belief, serves to further strengthen what
emotion has already magnified. When we choose to focus on beliefs that cause
us to fear, we perpetuate fear in our lives.

Fear takes many forms. It can manifest itself through a headache, a case
of flu, a depression; through anxiety, jealousy, anger, or hatred. It can
manifest itself through losing a job, breaking off with a lover, having an auto
accident. And it can manifest itself through the acts of others. We can see our
fears reflected back at us through the disturbing behavior of other people.

For me, this was the most difficult lesson to learn. Right from the start,
it made great sense to me that I created my own reality when it pertained to
the condition of my body, to the living environment I'd arranged for myself,
to the actions I took and the subsequent success or failure resulting from
them. I found it easy to accept the idea that these were realities I had created
for myself, and to accept the idea that insofar as I had fearful beliefs and
focussed on them, they would be reflected through these media. But only
recently have I come to see that the reality I create also pertains to the traits
and actions of others. Only recently have I come to see that when I repeatedly
decry the irresponsibility and scatteredness of others, I am voicing a fear in
myself that maybe, at bottom, I am like that too, despite my obvious
reliability and orderliness.

Seth uses the example of a very industrious individual who thinks of most others as being lazy and good for nothing. Though no one would ever think of *him* as lazy and good for nothing, this is what he fears he may be, and so drives himself mercilessly to escape from his feared notion of himself. And projects those traits outward onto others.

The point is, you cannot escape from fear this way. When you project it out there onto another person, you are not getting rid of it, for it still disturbs you. In fact, it may disturb you *more* than it would if it were manifested in some other way, for you don't feel you have control over other people's actions in the way you have control over your own. It makes you feel, once again, at the mercy of outside forces over which you have no control.

When we own up to our fear (whatever form it takes—anger, revulsion, hatred, disdain), then we can do something to lessen it. But when we continue to see it in others, then we only perpetuate and strengthen it. We will continue to encounter it. Casting aside this person or that is not the answer. There will always be another one who will agree to play our projected role. The only way we can "combat" our projected fears is to recognize them in ourselves, and then choose not to focus on them any more.

Which is not always as easy as it sounds! We get quite a charge out of feeling self-righteous, out of feeling superior, or even out of feeling put upon or misunderstood. It feels good not to have the responsibility for the projected behavior. Someone *else* has done it to us. We can really get into our anger, into our putdowns, into our martyrdom—someone else has done it to us, and we are innocent. But to the extent that we believe in innocence, we also believe in guilt, and therein lies the rub. On some level we feel guilty, for we recognize we created this reality for ourselves.

One of the bravest and most beneficial actions we can take, then, is to let go of our negative feelings for other people. To let go of the idea that those feelings we have were caused by that other person; to recognize that what we feel and what we perceive is our own responsibility, and that it does no good to berate the other person or to feel like a victim. It doesn't get us anywhere to blame others; in fact, it only holds us back, for it keeps us from recognizing fears that will continue getting in our way until we do.

In this exercise on letting go, begin by making a list in your journal of all the people toward whom you have negative feelings. Then, analyze each situation. Delineate the feelings you have for the person. Scorn? Distrust? Anger? Figure out what that person *did* to arouse those feelings in you. Ask yourself: what kind of a person would do something like that? Come up with some adjectives. (You might want to look at the long list in Exercise #12 for ideas.)

Now, look at the adjectives and see if they apply to you in any way, or, if the *opposite* applies to you. Are you reliable and orderly, while this person is irresponsible and scattered? Then it may well be that you fear those qualities in yourself. Otherwise, why would they disturb you? You may even discover in exploring your feelings further that you *envy* that person for "being able" to act that way when you are "unable" to. In any case, through this analysis, you should be able to understand that the feelings you have about this person are ones *you* generated. It is not that person's fault that you feel the way you do. You have no one to blame. The feelings are yours, so admit them. In the long run, you will feel better in taking responsibility for your own feelings than you will in projecting them onto others, for you will come to see that you do have a choice in how you feel. So long as you give your fears over to other people, you will never be able to overcome them.

Once you see how you caused the feelings you have for that person, and what is behind them, you should be ready to let go of them. You will recognize that the person triggered a fear in you; and it's the fear you have to work on and not waste your energy in feeling negatively toward that person. When you realize that, you can let go.

44

Self-Hypnosis

... You hypnotize yourself constantly with your own conscious thoughts and suggestions. The term hypnosis merely applies to a quite normal state in which you concentrate your attention, narrowing your focus to a particular area of thought or belief.

You concentrate with great vigor upon one idea, usually to the exclusion of others. It is a quite *conscious* performance. As such it also portrays the importance of belief, for using hypnosis you "force-feed" a belief to yourself, or one given to you by another—a "hypnotist;" but you concentrate all of your attention upon the idea presented [*The Nature of Personal Reality*, p. 77].

Seth likens the present to a pool of experience fed by many streams from both the past and the future. We choose to focus on one stream or another and, according to what we believe, adjust the current. If we believe the past was fraught with pain, then any stream of experience we focus on will be adjusted to that belief and flow into our present life from the past fraught with pain. If it seems to us that the past held no joys, it is simply that in the present we are concentrating on the negative to such a degree that we can allow no "distractions" to enter our mind and present another picture. Thus our beliefs hypnotize us into accepting and perpetuating a given world view.

There is, then, nothing magic about hypnosis. We are using it constantly, making suggestions in our head about the nature of reality. We give all of our attention to this internal chatter, not letting the outside world distract us. This limits our perspective—we see only what our beliefs lead us to see. What we see is the reality we have created for ourselves. When we allow new beliefs to come into our mind, we then talk to ourselves about them, concentrating on what they are telling us and seeing the world from a new perspective. Our reality changes as our beliefs change.

A staged hypnosis session affords dramatic proof of the idea that the point of power is in the present. When someone focuses very intensely on a simple statement, with no outside distractions to take her mind off what is happening here and now, you can clearly see that the belief she is focussing on, right before your eyes, becomes manifest. In a demonstration I saw, a woman was hypnotized and asked to concentrate on the suggestion that the index finger of her left hand, held straight up, would become so rigid and strong that no one would be able to bend it. And sure enough, after the hypnotic induction was over, two strong men tried their best to bend the woman's finger, but it would not budge—much to the woman's surprise, for she had been given the further suggestion that she would not remember what was said during hypnosis. But the belief given during hypnosis had taken effect anyway.

People tend to distrust hypnosis because they feel that they can be forced to accept suggestions they wouldn't ordinarily be open to. But this is not the case. No hypnotist can get us to accept beliefs we don't want to accept. We have to be open to them to begin with. The main difference between a formal, structured hypnosis session and the natural hypnosis that we have going on in our head all the time is that the formal hypnotism is more concentrated and more focussed and thus more quickly effective than natural hypnosis. We do not need another person to hypnotize us; we can do it ourselves. And self-hypnosis—formal, structured hypnosis—can be a powerful tool in reality-creating. Using it, we can quickly erase those sentences in our head that are causing us difficulties and replace them with positive, helpful ones.

Two ingredients necessary to hypnosis are intense narrow focus, and the absence of distractions. The more intense the focus and the fewer the distractions, the more effective it will be. In moments of panic, we often put ourselves into an intense hypnotic state, shutting out all distractions no matter how demanding they might ordinarily be, and focussing with great concentration and energy on the situation at hand. In this way we can quickly rally our bodies, through our new belief, into the necessary action—often an action we wouldn't have thought ourselves capable of under ordinary circumstances. The panic situation led us to suspend our usual belief in limited capabilities and to replace it with one that would get us out of the situation.

When we are panicky, of course, we are far from relaxed. But generally relaxation is helpful in bringing about a hypnotic condition because it quiets the body so the mind isn't constantly reminded of its messages. If we can fully relax and focus our attention completely on one belief to the exclusion of all others, we can be very effective in bringing new beliefs into manifestation. In fact, this can be one of the most effective methods of all, once we are aware of the beliefs we hold and the ones we want.

For this exercise, you are going to make a fifteen-minute self-hypnosis tape, giving yourself a formal structured hypnosis session. If you don't have a cassette player it is possible to imagine yourself in a hypnosis session, but it will be more difficult that way to achieve the intense concentration that you get using the tape.

You will begin the tape with suggestions for relaxation, and then focus on a single statement of belief that you want to actualize. Here is a suggested script for your hypnosis session, but you may want to make changes to suit your own conversational style. If you don't sound like "yourself," that can be distracting.

Lie down and relax. Take a deep breath. (*Pause.*) Now let the breath out slowly, and feel your body relax even more. (*Pause.*) Take another deep breath. (*Pause.*) And let it out slowly. (*Pause.*) You will continue to take deep breaths and to let them out slowly. And with each breath your body will become more relaxed.

(*Say each phrase that follows slowly, and pause in between.*) You can feel the relaxation coming into your toes... your toes are relaxing.... And now the relaxation is in the balls of your feet... and the balls of your feet are relaxing too.... And now the relaxation is moving up into your ankles... and they are relaxing on the bed.... The wave of relaxation is moving slowly... slowly... up your legs now.... The lower legs are relaxing... relaxing... letting go.... Feel the relaxation in your knees now as your knees totally relax.... Now the relaxation is moving up into your thighs... and you can feel them becoming like heavy weights sinking into the bed... totally... totally relaxed.... Now your pelvis is relaxing as waves of relaxation go through the muscles and your pelvis sinks into the bed.... And your buttocks too, are totally relaxed on the bed.... Now you can feel the relaxation in the small of your back where the spine meets the pelvis ... and the small of the back is totally, totally relaxed.... Now the relaxation is moving slowly up the spine and into the shoulder blades.... You can feel them on the bed, relaxed and sinking into the bed.... And your shoulders are relaxing too... sinking into the bed....

Now feel the relaxation spreading out from your shoulders and into your upper arms.... You can feel the muscles in your upper arms letting go... completely relaxing on the bed.... And the relaxation goes on down to the elbows and they relax too ... relax totally on the bed.... The relaxation reaches into your lower arms... and they relax and sink into the soft bed... totally relaxed.... And your wrists are relaxing too.... Now your hands are feeling that wave of relaxation and they are completely limp as they lie on the bed.... Now the wave of relaxation moves back up the arms and into the shoulders and on to the back of the neck, where the shoulders meet the neck, and you can feel that part of your body completely, completely give way and relax, limp, on the bed.... Now you can feel the relaxation going up the neck to the nape of the neck... and the nape of the neck is relaxing.... Now you can feel the relaxation spreading all over the scalp... all over the scalp you feel the tingling relaxation as your scalp totally relaxes.... Now the relaxation is spreading to your face... and you feel your forehead becoming smooth and relaxed.... And your eyes are soft and relaxed too.... You can feel the relaxation in your cheeks, as they become loose and relaxed in your face.... And around your mouth it is all relaxed...and your tongue is relaxed too.... And the relaxation is in your jaw...and your jaw feels slack and loose and relaxed.... And now...all of your body...is to-tally...totally...relaxed...sinking into the bed...in delicious relaxation.... You are totally relaxed.

Now that you have yourself relaxed, you are ready to make your suggestion. Be sure that it is a positive, unlimiting one. For instance, "I am getting over my shyness, my shyness is going away," will only remind you of the belief that you are shy and is counterproductive. Say instead, "I feel calm and relaxed when talking to people," or something like that. The rest of your tape might go like this:

Now you are in a relaxed state...a deeply relaxed state...and your mind is completely open and alert.... You are able to concentrate completely on this belief statement.... You are going to suspend all other beliefs for the moment and completely accept this statement.... Focussing completely on this statement will activate your biological and psychological patterns...and they will then bring this belief into reality.... All you need to do is listen closely...to concentrate on this belief.... That is all you need to do, is to focus your attention completely on this belief.... In doing so you will be setting the mechanisms into motion which will bring into reality this belief.... Focus your attention completely, now, on this statement.

Now say the statement slowly and emphatically, over and over again. You might emphasize different words each time so that in listening you will be kept alert by these slight changes in intonation, or you may want to phrase the suggestion in different ways. But use only one idea, and say it over and over again until you have used up about thirteen minutes of the tape. You might remind yourself every minute or two that focussing on this statement will activate the mechanisms to bring the belief into reality.

Then for the last two minutes of the tape, bring yourself slowly out of your relaxed, hypnotic state:

You have now put a new belief into activation.... That new belief is now a part of your reality.... It is a part of your life...you have done what is necessary to activate that belief and it is now a part of your reality.... That is all you need to do to make that belief a reality.... You don't have to think about it any more... You know that, from your point of power in the present, you have brought into activation that belief.... It will soon be manifest in your every day life.... You need do no more.... Now you can slowly wake yourself up.... It is just as if you had a relaxing sleep, and you feel great.... Full of energy.... Your mind is clear and alert, and your body is filled with energy.... You feel very calm and filled with peace...and confidence in yourself that you do create your own reality.... You are waking up now feeling good all over.... Waking up, full of vitality and the joy that life brings.... On the count of five you will open your eyes and be fully awake.... Number one...number two...number three...number four...number five. Fully awake and raring to go!

If you intend to play the tape before going to sleep at night, suggest instead that you will fall into your usual sleep, that you will sleep well, and awaken refreshed.

Play this tape often, and when you have actualized the belief on it, erase that part of the tape and incorporate a new suggestion to work on.

45

Belief Assignment #9

You will not find yourself by running from teacher to teacher, from book to book. You will not meet yourself through following any *specialized* method of meditation. Only by looking quietly within the self that you know can your own reality be experienced [*Seth Speaks*, pp. 413–4].

For this final belief assignment, focus on the constructive beliefs you would like to cultivate in yourself. First, make a list in your journal of *results* you would like to see manifested, both psychological and physical. One result might be increased creativity. Another one might be a higher-paying job. After you have noted these down, think of several beliefs that would lead to each result. Make sure they are not limiting in some way, and that they do not conflict with other beliefs you have listed.

Now see if you can combine some of these beliefs, or subsume them under a more general belief that would do service for two or three of your goals. Keep doing this until you end up with one or two powerful belief statements which you can easily remember. Affirm these statements several times a day.

46

The God of You

There is no personal God-individual in Christian terms, and yet you do have access to a portion of All That Is, a portion highly attuned to you.... There is a portion of All That Is directed and focussed within each individual, residing within each consciousness. Each consciousness is, therefore cherished and individually protected. This portion of overall consciousness is individualized within you.

The personality of God is generally conceived as a one-dimensional concept based upon man's knowledge of his own psychology. What you prefer to think of as God is, again, an energy gestalt or pyramid consciousness. It is aware of itself as being...the smallest seed.... This portion of All That Is that is aware of itself as you, that is focussed within your existence can be called upon for help when necessary. This portion is also aware of itself as something more than you. *This portion that knows itself as you, and as more than you, is the personal God, you see...* [*The Seth Material*, p. 270].

In *The God of Jane*, Jane Roberts tells what inspired her to use that title for her book.

We share the world with others, but portions of it carry personal significance. We see them as no one else does. So it was for me that morning. No one else was watching what I watched from my own personal viewpoint. I felt as if I were being privileged to view a beginning of the world—or my edge of it. Or, I thought suddenly, it was like seeing a new corner of your own psyche transformed into trees, grass, flowers, fog and sky—a hopeful, magical, ever-coming-into-existence part of the psyche that we'd forgotten or I'd forgotten. I felt as if I were viewing that part of myself that I'm always pursuing, the part that is as clear-eyed as a child, fleet, at one with its own knowing; the part that exists apart from daily concerns; the part that was my direct connection with the universe; the part that represented that section of the universe from which I emerged in each moment of my life. And in that moment I named it the God of Jane... I didn't know if I was turning into the morning, or the morning was turning into me, but I did know that *The God of Jane* would be the title of my book. [*The God of Jane*, pp. 64–5.]

The more she thought about the idea, the more she liked it, for it presupposed an intimate connection between each person and the universe, and also made a distinction between one's own private "God" and the God of the Universe or All That Is. She wrote

> For instance, when I use the phrase "the God of Jane," I'm referring to or trying to contact that portion of the universe that is forming *me* —that is turning some indefinable divinity into this living temporal flesh. I'm not trying to contact the God of Abraham, for instance, or the Biblical Christ, or the inexplicable power behind all of reality. My intent is more humble than that, more personal, more specific: I want to contact that tiny portion of All That Is that forms *my* image, that transforms itself or part of itself into my experience ... That God of Jane must be continuous with the entire cloth of divinity, but I'm not asking that the entire attention of All That Is be turned in my direction. Besides, this would be quite unnecessary anyway, since according to Seth, any portion of All That Is contains the knowledge of all of its other parts [pp. 65–6.]

Jane told her friend Sue Watkins about her idea, and Sue was quite taken with it. A few days later she sent Jane a poem she had written, interpreting the idea for herself:

THE GOD OF SUE
by Susan M. Watkins
With Thanks to *The God of Jane*

She rides inside a dirty car,
one fender bent in a tinfoil sneer.
This is Her chariot of the sun.
Her world travels
(just like they guessed)
on the back of a grandfather turtle.
Pretty funny, my dear
God.

She walks down village streets and hides
Her God-ness fervently inside
Her pocketbook.
And sometimes She forgets
and accidentally lets
Her checkbook balance by itself,
or thinks about the fall and makes
the trees turn red and gold too soon.
Five demerits, my dear
God.

She thought the God of Man
kind was a jerk.

128

She loves desire,
She loves to love,
but as far as being loved, ah, well—
sometimes She simply isn't
sure She wants
the person who comes with it.
(She doesn't like to cook.)

Ah-ha! But this explains the
reason why
She threw aside
the book about
the God of Man—
the stupid S.O.B. eschewed
the use
of his own complimentary piece
of flesh!
Good thinking, my dear
God.

Once, after growing a fishy type
of thing into a
functioning adult, She said,
"I don't do anything
that's right."
Quite frankly, even
the God of Man
would laugh at that.

It took until She saw
that having faith was not
the snap
that all those martyrs claimed
they had while being stuck
with arrows or what-have-you.
In fact,
it took much less
than that—Too bad for them, by God

The God of Sue created the Earth.
I saw her do it all Myself. [pp.67–8.]

After I read Sue's poem in *The God of Jane*, I too got inspired, and one day batted this down in my journal:

The God of Nancy
Rides in an orange and mud-streaked jeep
Top down, barrelling bumpily over cane road
Looking out at the lush green hills
Her special hills

Does anyone else see them quite that way?
God, no.

Arrives panting from four flights
In class—late
Takes a seat in the semicircle of chairs
Her students have started without her
and hardly notice her arrival—
How dear they seem
Does anyone else see them quite that way?
God, no.

A student comes to see her
In her windowless frigid office
Shelves piled high with teaching materials
Which bespeak the place's only purpose
A repository of information
With her as synthesizer
Does anyone else see things quite that way?
God, no.

Gets home at five
Cats appear as if they'd known ahead
A walk on the beach
Slow, many pauses to look back
towards Haleiwa
or out at the surfers
She is continually aware of the sand underfoot
of the brightly-colored coral
of the smell and the sound of the sea
Does anyone else savor quite that way?
God, no.

Sits on the screened porch
Sky darkening
Sipping and smoking
Listening and
Thinking
Watching thoughts pass by
Noticing the way they change from
one to another
Experiencing them from a different perspective
Does anyone else think quite that way?
God, no.

Goes into her studio
Stacked with work
Sensuous, elegant, simple
yet strong
She looks through her sketches
One catches her eye

And soon she is working
Transferring to cloth
Her image.
Next she will sew
and then she will stuff
Savoring the wait
Before she'll see
It grown, organic,
In three dimensions
Does anyone else create in this way?
God, no.

As you can see, the two poems are entirely different, each reflecting an intensely personal focus on existence, each viewed from a different center. As the final exercise in this book, see if you can put into words what it is like to be *you*, the creator of your own uniquely personal reality, a personification of that portion of All That Is that is focussed through you, the focus that is the point of intersection between the inner and the outer worlds.

Write your own poem entitled "The God of Me" (or your name), and see what happens as the images get flowing. What *is* it that makes you so unique? Your private experience seems so ordinary to you, yet it is like no one else's. To everyone else it is extraordinary. Revel in the *extraordinary* self that is you!

Afterword

If you've thumbed this far, you already know what this canny, wonderfully practical book is all about. From the rather hefty array of Jane Roberts's work, Nancy Ashley has gleaned Seth's essential ideas and distilled them into 46 concise chapters. For veteran Seth fans, then, this volume is a dazzlingly valuable reminder of points that are healthy to bear in mind. And for anyone who hasn't yet read the original books, Ms. Ashley does a superb job of presenting Seth's ideas clearly and comprehensively in "crash course" form.

If that were *all* she'd done, this book would still be worth the price. But *Create Your Own Reality* also offers a series of psychological exercises. Some are Seth's; others arise from Ms. Ashley's own impulses and experiences. All are equally useful, equally liberating. If you've paused to try any of them, you may already have been rewarded with changes in your everyday life. New zest and energy, for example. Or exuberant Technicolor dreams. Or (as in my case) people in the street becoming happier, friendlier, and better-looking—literally overnight.

But after the first thrill of success and a string of easy breakthroughs, the changes may suffer a slowdown. After an all-too-brief spiritual high, you may strike lodes of unexpected pain or uncover a bewildering array of negative beliefs, seemingly too many to cope with. Worse yet, you may feel yourself relapsing into the reality you thought you had escaped by doing those exercises in the first place! Why the diminishing returns? Or were your first achievements just beginner's luck?

I asked such questions myself. That's why I asked to write an Afterword, to reassure readers who may have run into the same kind of problems.

You see, when Prentice-Hall mailed me the manuscript of *Create Your Own Reality* for editing, I was very much at sea (metaphorically speaking) in one particular area of my emotional life. After doing a number of the exercises in this book, I experienced some surprising and very welcome changes—yet still didn't find myself any closer to shore (as it were) in the *one* area where I had most hoped to see progress! I felt deeply betrayed—by whom or by what, I wasn't sure. Then suddenly, amid all the grief and frustration, up popped the hitherto-hidden beliefs that had been keeping me (so to speak) dead in the water.

Not too surprisingly, most of them were fears and doubts: *What if I get rolled in the surf? What if pirates are lurking behind those palm trees? And*—most startling of all!—*what's so terrific about that particular stretch of dry land?* To my sincere astonishment, I found I really wasn't wholeheartedly eager for an amphibious landing on the sands of my long-sought goal. Rather, I wanted more time to paddle around, enjoy the rocking of the waves, and maybe let the current carry me to an even better landfall.

And so, what first appeared to be an utter failure turned out to be a kind of sneaky success.

Which brings me to one of the really neat things about *Create Your Own Reality:* There simply isn't any way to do these exercises incorrectly! If you get absolutely zilch out of a given set of instructions, that doesn't mean you're doing anything wrong. Rather, it suggests you're in the lee of a rather deeply rooted belief, one that is now ready for your conscious investigation. The human psyche doesn't always travel the shortest distance between two points, and if your beliefs aren't all pulling in the same direction, you may well find yourself bafflingly becalmed, just as I was.

By itself, then, this book will not take you to Honolulu. Nor is it some kind of psychic aspirin tablet to assuage your multidimensional growing pains. What it *will* do is help you hoist the anchors that keep you from flowing with your life's Larger Currents; from drifting naturally, inevitably and yes, *peacefully* toward whatever land that will best fulfill your purposes—or (and here's another sneaky part!) to whatever shore you *think* you want to reach. As I discovered the hard way, one's values and goals, one's "itinerary" and "travel plans" are sets of beliefs too.

You can change those beliefs, of course, just as easily as I'm going to cast loose these nautical metaphors. As the exercises in this book will quickly demonstrate, beliefs can be every bit as varied, enjoyable, and potentially creative as the clothes we wear. And that, O Best Beloved, is yet another lesson that springs from the pages of this book: That you can select your beliefs just as easily as you select clothes from your closet every morning.

This beliefs-as-wardrobe analogy isn't strictly accurate, of course, because belief-wise, "every morning" is right now. Also, your Belief Closet is literally infinite, with more racks, styles, fabrics, and colors that you'll ever have a chance to try on. Nevertheless, the comparison's still useful because beliefs—just like clothes—can be both helpful and limiting at the same time. If you insist on nothing but blue-jean beliefs, you won't be admitted to too many fancy restaurants. But then, if you're all gussied up in dinner-jacket beliefs, you won't get invited to too many volleyball games. Obviously, you want to be able to change beliefs where and when it seems appropriate. But this is where things can get a bit tricky.

Before leaving on a week's vacation, a couple I know left their very young son with his grandmother and told the boy (who had never before dressed himself) to be sure to put on clean underwear every day. You guessed it: when they returned home, the kid was waddling around in seven pairs of underwear, one on top of the other. So it is with beliefs: All too often (though mostly for self-protection), we overdress. Then we wonder why physical existence gets so sweaty at times, why we can't move freely and spontaneously. Even worse, we start to envy those young kids down the street who seem to run around in hardly any beliefs at all—and get away with it!

In short, trying *on* new beliefs demands that you take other beliefs *off*. (Students of philosophy will recall that celebrated seventeenth-century stripper Rene Descartes, inventor of the fundamental undergarment known as *Cognito ergo sum*.) But it's best to go easy: At one point while reading this book, I worried that I might be hobbled by all sorts of limiting beliefs and became impatient with trying to discover them one by one. Instead, I resolved to unplug the whole lot of them with one single, all-purpose belief statement—*only helpful and dynamic beliefs will have any effect in my life*—and delivered it as per the instructions in Exercise #44.

What's wrong with that? Well, for about two weeks, my thoughts were filled with flapping black negativities that no longer had any place to roost. On top of that, it turns out that just as there are bridge beliefs (as explained in Exercise #40), so there are also relatively inert "buffer" beliefs that keep contradictory impulses in the psyche from crashing into one another. In effect, the forementioned affirmation yanked away all my cotton wadding. So for a while, I had a great many conflicting values and opinions sliding around loose and going *crumpf* into one another. It took me some time to sweep up all the psychological debris.

The point is, no matter how inappropriate the beliefs you and I have on right now, we *once* selected them for very good reasons. There was once a time when they made us feel warm and confident and capable. Naturally, times and fashions change. Beliefs are particularly easy to outgrow and wear out, but that doesn't mean we were numbskulls for having adopted them in the first place. So if your beliefs are obsolete, in other words, don't be too hard on yourself.

And don't be too hard on *them*, either. Any belief you ever held still merits a certain respect—if only because thoughts are living, conscious constructions in their own right. Thus, it is not proper to "annihilate" or "kill" a belief that you want to get rid of. What you want to do is engineer a graceful, diplomatic parting of the ways: *Hey, belief about such-and-such, you're off duty now. Go punch out, put up your feet, relax, and enjoy your retirement.* Or, if you're more formal: *Dear belief, you have guided me and supported me, exactly as I created you to do. Now, though, the circumstances that gave you birth no longer apply. So please depart, for your further development as well as mine.*

Okay, now you're ready to select a replacement belief that's more rewarding. But this is where things can get tricky again.

If people took the same care in shopping for new beliefs as they do in scrutinizing the new European fashions, doubtless we'd all be better "fitted" for everyday life. But until someone comes along with a *Whole Belief Catalog* or introduces a line of designer beliefs whose patterns you can copy, you'll have to use your own best judgment. How do you choose beliefs that will match the life you want to live? Easy! Next time you go to select from the Belief Closet, turn to Exercise #15 and #34. For me, these two Memory Refreshers sharpen the image of what life can be at its best. After that, it's easy to select new beliefs suitable for such occasions.

Cultivating this kind of discrimination lets you squeeze yet another insight from the beliefs-as-garments analogy: *You don't have to wear "traditional" beliefs just because your family, mate, or friends do.* You can pass up the sacrificial hair shirt beliefs and the defensive chain-mail beliefs of the Middle Ages, along with the celluloid collar beliefs and whalebone corset beliefs of your grandparents. You can politely exchange those beliefs that Mom and Dad gave you for your twelfth birthday for some new ones that really fit you. (In actuality, there's no such thing as a second-hand belief, because *any* belief you hold is entirely your own creation—an extremely skillful replica, maybe, but your own brand-new handiwork, regardless.)

You may even find you don't need a whole new belief wardrobe after all. Maybe you just need to alter the beliefs you have, to make them more comfortable and a little less restrictive. But either way, there will come a certain period of adjustment before physical reality falls in line with the new belief—and this period of "alterations" can be lengthy, and sometimes discouraging.

An old legend has it that Rome actually *was* built in a day, but then caught all kinds of flak from the housing inspectors. That's why you want to give a new belief enough time to take effect. After you adopt any new affirmation, it may seem to vanish—but that's only because you're wearing it! You may not be aware of it again until you glance into a psychological mirror and see how great you look. (For one such mirror, see Exercise #43.) And until that new belief gets broken in and becomes second nature, your emotions and imagination will tend to act as gyroscopes, making it hard for you to change direction. You may even miss your old belief when you find yourself, out of habit, reaching into a pocket that's no longer there. All perfectly normal! You may even get so caught up in the drama of the resulting events that you forget what it is you affirmed in the first place. (But that's fine too. If you're constantly aware that a movie is only a movie, it's not much fun, is it?)

But sooner or later the changes, however minor, *will* come. Then you can adopt even spiffier beliefs to go with that new reality—and make the change in increments, if not in one fell swoop. But practicing the exercises in this book can help you become a quick-change artist, speeding the whole process considerably.

For example, when I began the first draft of this Afterword, I was feeling quite ill—mainly, I assumed, because I'd just spent the entire Labor Day weekend in a frenzied marathon of typing to finish a project that had been my number-one priority since June. My body was winding down from a long-term adrenaline alert; and that, together with an unseasonable heat wave, were perfectly valid reasons to feel wretched.

But then I decided to get in touch with the feeling-tones that Ms. Ashley covers in her very first exercise. Soon, I could sense not only the wellsprings of past and future health, but also the rather creative way in which I was diverting *present* energy into these unpleasant symptoms. Basically, finishing up that three-month project had left a kind of power vacuum in my daily schedule. Now, strong impulses that I'd had to deny for several weeks—creative, emotional, professional—were all vying for that vacant top slot, snapping and snarling at one another.

I reconciled the spat by putting my professional impulse—namely, writing this Afterword—back in first place. Almost immediately I felt physically better and, in a state of pleasurable creativity and high enthusiasm, quickly completed the first draft of the words you're reading now.

A couple of last reminders: These are just some of the discoveries that *Create Your Own Reality* has prompted me to stumble on—so far! But the various analogies I've been spinning are *themselves* beliefs, of course—and just like any other beliefs, they are a means of looking at reality and of creating it; and *not* to be confused with reality itself. You're welcome to share my discoveries, but don't assume they're necessarily the same kind of insights that this book will elicit in *you*. If you don't roll up your own belief-sleeves, kick off your belief-shoes and devote some real energy to these exercises, you're going to be selling Ms. Ashley short—and shortchanging yourself as well.

Tam Mossman
Philadelphia, Pennsylvania

Index